T0316528

Nothing to See Here

Nothing to See Here

Edited by Hilda Twongyeirwe

FEMRITE - Uganda Women Writers Association
P.O. Box 705, Kampala
Tel: +256 414 543943 / +256 772 743943
Email: info@femriteug.org
www.femriteug.org

Copyright © FEMRITE - Uganda Women Writers Association 2015

First Published 2015

All rights reserved. No part of this publication may be reproduced, stored in retrieval system, or transmitted in any form, or by any means electronic, mechanical, photocopying, recording or otherwise without written permission of the publisher or the contributors who hold copyright to their individual stories.

Cover Picture – Juliet Kushaba
Cover and Layout design by Bonnetvanture T Asiimwe
proxyconceptsconsult@gmail.com

Printed by:
Good News Printing Press Ltd.
P.O. Box 21228 Kampala, Uganda
Tel: +256 414 344897
E-mail: info@goodnewsprinting.co.ug

Nothing to See Here

Stories of the 5th
Residency for African Women Writers

FEMRITE PUBLICATIONS LIMITED
KAMPALA

Acknowledgement

FEMRITE appreciates the input of all partners and colleagues who have been part of the process to make this publication possible.

The writers for sharing their stories and their lives with FEMRITE. The Swedish Institute and African Women's Development Fund, for supporting both The Regional Residency for African Women Writers and the publication of this anthology. The Karavan Magazine, for being keen about developing African women writers and for working with FEMRITE to implement the Regional Residency Project.

Table of Contents

ALWAYS THE HEAD

Melissa Kiguwa

We chew over every piece of small talk until it sits like stale curd at the back of our mouths. Through our ruminations, we stumble upon my father's name (father defined as the one who gave sperm and five years). Stretched on the bed, I put the telephone on the pillow and place my ear on top of it so that I do not have to hold it anymore. I think, mostly, the name Ngenyo is useless to me at this point in my life, I say into the mouthpiece. I do not know what it means or where it comes from. And I get so embarrassed when the questions, 'Where is your name from? What does your name mean?' come and I have no answers. I cannot be this old and still be dealing with identity shame.

I can hear her smile. You could try and find out, she tells me. Then we both laugh. What hadn't we done to try and reach out to my father's side? Results had yielded stalkers masquerading as cousins, clan meetings convened without me to begin the process of resuming a long-standing ritual, and truths about my own grandfather who had long ago disowned everybody in his family and refused to give me any information. She speaks after our laughter has subsided: at least Facebook brought about some interesting results.

About two years ago I found a Ruth Ngenyo on Facebook and we began communicating. She was feminist and radical and we took to one another right away. At that same time I had just received acceptance for a fellowship at the University of Witwatersrand and she was one of the fellowship instructors. We figured it fate and chatted on and off about school, romance, finding one's place, and this lost tribe of people called the Ngenyos. Even she had no linkages to our people, and I accepted that perhaps my people were like that: brilliant and the most clichéd type of isolationist.

My mother visited South Africa that same year and took along baby clothes as a present for Ruth's expectant sister. I remember her nervousness before she set off on the trip. Solo, I know she is having a boy, but I bought a yellow baby suit . . . I just know how you feminists are. I figured if I got the baby something blue, Ruth and her sister may think I am trying to socialise the baby into mainstream masculinity. I laughed at her words until the credit on the phone ran out.

Ahh, Ngenyo, Ngenyo, my mother interrupts my thoughts. We have tried and tried and tried to get your grandfather to give us more information. To give us a link, a name, even a number—anything that would give you an anchor. I sigh into the phone.

During my childhood, my mother and I talked constantly about Joseph Ngenyo. I have memories of him before their separation, a quiet man with glasses that remind me of pictures of Patrice Lumumba. Then there are the memories of him after their separation; these are patchy. Was it really him, flighty and hostile, banging at our door in London with police officers behind him? I visited him about five times after they separated, each time meeting him in a new residence. Once in someone's garage, another time in a friend's guest room, and the other three places are silhouettes I cannot place. At the time, I tried to understand him and why he left. And when I wanted to move back to London many years later, I remember his letter, a rejection of the daughter who has his eyes. My mother would tell me all kinds of stories trying to convince me I was still loved and appreciated and wanted by this Houdini of a man she had married.

The pictures of my mother during this time show a shell. Her cheeks sunken, legs the size of twigs. She laughs when she sees I still carry those pictures in my wallet. You surely are a weird child, Solo. Why you would want to keep pictures of such an ugly woman! Look, you can even see the bones under my eyes! And she laughs again, probably because these days her cheeks are full and his name rarely comes up.

I do not know when we stopped referring to Joseph Ngenyo outside of family reunions with aunties who had not seen me in years. I suppose his name became scarce because we had other things to do. Full-time jobs, cousins giving birth, friends whose families were disintegrating. We had little time to ruminate over people who leave. I learnt, first from my mother, to fill the memory of emptiness through one-way tickets to places further and further away from the cradle of betrayal.

As though hearing my thoughts straying, my mother asks whether I will change both of my names to make Solome into something more traditional and African-y. I laugh. No, seriously Solo, she says, I know it's what's hip with the pan-Africanists. I'm just waiting to read a poem somewhere by Olumide Ngenyo formerly known as Solome. I laugh again, this time from somewhere deep.

Olumide is so far from my reality, Mama! If you ever read a poem by Olumide Ngenyo formerly known as Solome, please give me a nice big *mscheeew* slap over the phone. She giggles.

But, like many lessons learnt from my mother, I understand that simply because someone is attached to you does not mean they want all the details. I wonder about telling her of my intention to hyphenate my name. Well, I start shyly, I know it is about ten years overdue, but I've been thinking about hyphenating my last name.

Really? she asks. Well, yeah. Everyone knows me as Ngenyo, but again, it is just a sound. Consonants and vowels strung together, no meaning. But Chindama, well, that is the name of the man who raised me. Who played dad and who has seen me grow. While it is still too patrilineal for my liking, I would like to take dad's name (dad defined as the one who raised me).
Wow, she says. I don't know if I ever thought those words would come from your mouth. She chuckles: the both of you gave me hell you know. The way you would fight each other . . . and now come to find out you're really the same person. Stubborn and hard-headed. I laugh and ask, that is not such a bad thing, is it? She says, I suppose not. It has gotten us this far, right? I nod as though she can see me. It has gotten us far . . . Ngenyo-Chindama. I say, it all seems so ceremonial, changing my name. It seems like a lot of work. I was thinking of just getting rid of the Ngenyo altogether. Maybe taking on your name. Mayanja-Chindama.

I hear her nodding. Yeah, she says, your younger cousin did that. We all know her dad is useless, so when she decided to take our family name no one said anything. Now she is Agnes Rurangirwa. But she had that insight quite young. The problem in your case is people have known you as Ngenyo since you were a child. You know in school no one knew my name was Peace, they called me Sarah Mulungi. When I left school I went by Peace Mayanja, and after I got married to your father I became

Peace Ngenyo. And then I got married to dad and now I am Peace Chindama. I've lost a lot of connections and contacts simply because people cannot find me. They do not know my name.

I want to process through the depth of what she has just said. Constantly changing identities. Not knowing one's name. Loss. But she prompts me to continue speaking to my naming process and I put my questions on the backburner for a later conversation. What of Solome? she asks. Are you going to keep Solome?

I have definitely thought about changing Solome, especially when I first began attending Pan-African events. She laughs. Seriously, mom! The way they Malcolm X us into believing anything that seems relatively mainstream is somehow a false consciousness. But, really . . . I pause, trying to collect my thoughts, and then shift positions on the bed before continuing, I think some things are a bit deeper than that. When you named me Solome, you did so with intention. The skin of sound is sometimes thick and melanin-rich. And I have fallen into the sound, or rather the skin.

My God, she interrupts, where did you learn to be so melodramatic? I ignore her and continue, from me, Solome, to you, Peace, whose mother named you a Biblical skin, to your mother, Juliet, who was grafted a skin of Latin derivatives. Three generations bound in a grip so tight only we can see a reflection of something other than oppressed. I see it: the whiteness, the syllables that pray difficult on kinsmen's lips. I continue, how can I change my name? As though I am ashamed of your decisions? She interrupts me, but it was Malcolm X who said he does not know his name because it was a slave name, hence the X. That his father did not know his name either and his father's father because they were given names of the white man. There's that story too, Solo, the story of erasure. I tell her, my story lies in you naming me. While it may not speak to nativity the way some would like to romanticise it, it does speak to our reality. Of passage, movement, inspiration, and yes, of too much luzungu in our mouths. But that, too, is part of the story.

She is quiet and I wonder if the international package I bought on my SIM card has run out. She begins so softly I hardly hear her at first. That is interesting. You know I was just reading about a tribe, I do not remember which, but they have a practice that is so interesting . . . She stops talking and I smile. I know her well enough to understand her need for affirmative prodding, a reminder her words are being listened to. How so? I ask softly. She pauses and sucks in air before she continues. Well, before a mother gives birth she goes to a tree. I am not sure how this tree is picked, but it is picked and it is her duty to put her ear up to the tree and listen. Inside the tree is her child's song, and as she listens to the song she begins singing and memorising it. When the baby is born, she sings her child's song. And that is how it is that, anytime the child achieves a milestone or any rite of passage, his or her song is sung. I read that and I said, my goodness! I would have loved to have had such a song. If only . . . well, anyway, even when the child messes up, you know, maybe becomes a thief or is just doing things that go against the codes of the family, the entire family calls the child home and they sing the song to the child. It is then the child's choice as to whether she or he wants to leave the path he or she is on and return to goodness . . .

She finishes her story and I sigh, that is so beautiful.

Yeah, I thought so too. I remembered it when you told me the reason you wanted to keep the name Solome. I smile into the phone, well, mama, can I sing you a song? I may not have heard it in a tree, but can I sing you a song? Please, she says. I begin singing the chorus to Mahalia Jackson's 'Precious Lord Take My Hand,' one of her favourites. She hums the harmony. Thanks, Solo. Well, you know it is getting quite late this side and I know your credit is about to finish. Love you. I love you too, Mama, I say. We get off the phone, her more than three thousand miles away and me here in someone else's bed. I climb off the bed with a great sigh and stretch a bit. Downstairs, I hear the television on and I debate going to sleep or checking on Moses. I decide on going downstairs.

Moses is asleep on the couch and is not disturbed when I switch off the television. I watch him sprawled like an unending question and try to figure out where I can squeeze myself in. I settle down next to him, now the both of us curled into a pair. These are my favourite moments, my head on his chest, the peace. I feel the slow rise and fall of his chest, the deep rumble of his snore. Skin to skin, the only thing clearly distinct between us are the rhythms of our heartbeats and even that harmonises after some time. With his mouth open, I imagine a dark-hollowed tunnel where steam engines get lost. Engines chug and puff their way to his lungs. I hear the *choo-choo* all the way down to his stomach. I imagine us catching a red-eye flight. Destination: beyond the limitation of boundaries and borders. But even I know it is never that simple. He shifts and sighs while pulling me closer, babe, I can hear you thinking.

We have sleeping rules. Rule one: When asleep, politics is suspended. To be more specific, my part-time sociologist is supposed to go on vacation. Sometimes it works, but Moses and I are babies of Diaspora and migration, so, to me, our moments of suspended debating are really moments of building home with each other, through each other. He calls it primal connectedness. I think of it as some form of catharsis in exodus.

I fall asleep snuggled next to him and dream that a leopard with a baby's face is running towards me. I am mesmerised by her face, both childlike and hideous. One eye in the middle of her forehead, a snake's tongue protruding from her mouth, and whiskers curled at her chin. I know she is not bad, but I know she will kill me. As she reaches close enough to pounce on me I hear her purring a lullaby. With her claws she rips into my stomach and pulls out my intestines in the shape of a wedding ring. Moses' phone rings and I wake up with a start. I pick up the phone and see the letter T. It's a name I frequently see calling and getting rejected. Moses takes the phone from me, turns down the ringer, and puts the phone in his pocket. Why don't you pick it? I ask. Ah, it will be a long call and I'm tired, he says, stroking my cheek.

When I awake in the morning, Moses has already left for work. He usually makes us breakfast and I find a covered plate on the kitchen table with a note. *Baby, got called into a surprise early-morning meeting at the office and didn't want to wake you. Wish I could have had breakfast with you! Love you! M.* I smile at my sheer luck of having met someone as much a shameless romantic as I, and then, grabbing a slice of bread from my plate, I hurry upstairs to get ready.

On my desk at the office, I find my copy of Dr. Sylvia Tamale's reader, *African Sexualities,* which I had lent to a colleague. Morning, Solome! Thank God it's a Friday. And thanks so much for letting me have the book. I got the information I needed, my colleague says, lingering by the door. I know he did not read anything in the book; he often asks to borrow my things to somehow see if I will give him more attention than I do. There is one other person seated in the room and she makes deliberate coughing noises at him. He, aloof and persistent, does not leave until I say, I'm glad you got what you needed. Have a good day.

I look down at the reader, dog-eared and highlighted all over. I flip through the book again and land on a short story by Chimamanda Adichie that I always seem to keep coming back to. There is a line in the story on how she wonders whether Yale taught her white American lover to speak authoritatively on things he does not know. The line always makes me pause. It always makes me think of the US indoctrination of *fake it 'til you make it,* which sort of forces one to claim space even if they are not entitled to it. I think of how being indoctrinated into such an empire has affected me. But, mostly, I wonder if Moses has ever asked himself such questions of me.

At lunch, I meet with a friend who analyses my current relationship in a detached, clinical way, as if she has forgotten I have feelings and personal insecurities. Moses is really a catch, she says. Handsome, educated, successful. I mean, every educated Ugandan woman is trying to meet such a guy. Perhaps if we all had that American accent of yours we would stand a chance. I stare at my plate. You really believe the only reason Moses is attracted to me is because of my accent? She looks at me incredulously. Honestly the only reason you were able to meet him is because of your Diaspora privilege!

I look at my friend, feeling at the same time offended and amused. Offended because I never know what weight to give to such comments and amused because, to this friend, all things I do and say are viewed within the lens of Diaspora privilege. But the nuances within desire and power are too complex for me to examine during lunch on a Friday, so instead I joke, honey with this face and booty, regardless of what country I'm in, I'll never have a problem getting successful, handsome dates. She smiles at me stiffly.

Moses has a particular facial expression when I bring up such interactions. It is as though I have squeezed pili-pili into his mouth. We are home from work but are both feeling too lazy to go out. He is seated on the sofa and my head is on his lap. Miles Davis is playing on the stereo and Moses uses his index finger to tap elongated rhythms on my forehead. I know he wants to watch MSNBC. He has a crush on Rachel Maddow that grows stronger whenever he hears her dissecting Republican rhetoric and Obama's budget. I am not invested enough in US policy to consider it a fair competition.

He looks at me and stops tapping. Privilege is a heavy word, he says. I think these things have more depth than whatever she is jealous about. I think the real underlying point to take away from the conversation is that you need new friends. I remind him it is not just this friend. That we are immersed in a global culture that values some bodies more than others. Valued bodies, if not white, tend to speak a certain kind of English. They tend to be groomed bourgeoisie in a certain kind of way. And when you can play the game, the playing field is completely different. I tell him it is important to know the ways in which cultural power structures rate one's body and experiences as valuable because it does so at the expense of others. Oh my god, he says rolling his eyes. Edward Said called, he wants his thesis back. I smile and roll my eyes back at him. I hear his stomach rumble and suggest we make something to eat. I tell him he's on chopping duty.

Making our way to the fridge only reveals a premature decision. We shop for groceries on Saturday mornings and so our Friday night fridge selection is usually dismal. There are two tomatoes, one onion, a small bottle of hot sauce standing beside withered mangoes and avocadoes, a bottle of red wine, several old eggplants and some hardened cheese, and half of a green pepper. The cut pepper lies next to Irish potatoes and a clove of garlic. We spend some time discussing what edible miracle we can conjure up with the ingredients in front of us. We could try to make a mango glazed sauce like we saw on the Cooking Network the other day, he says. I smile: Baby, this is not a mango. It is a fossil. We cannot cook with Palaeolithic remnants. Maybe we should try a wine-based sauce? He ponders awhile before saying, wine-based sauce on eggplant and cheese? Alright, let's try it. If it's horrible we'll feed it to my brother. You know he eats anything.

He takes the onion, green pepper, and tomatoes out of the fridge, washes them and begins chopping. I laugh, those are too big! With lips pressed together in concentration, he continues chopping chunks too big for me to cook with. You gave me the small chopping board, he complains as his eyes take on a mischievous look I know too well. You know, I am an African man. You need to give me more respect. Oh? And the big chopping board gives you more respect? I ask. He is now chopping tomatoes. Of course . . . taking up space is what I do, he says as he leans forward to kiss my cheek. I smile and ask, taking up space? When did you become such an imperialist? I'm quite sure we never would have gotten together if I knew. He laughs that deep laugh that made me fall in love with him. I've always been. I just lied when we first met. I chuckle and continue seasoning the diced eggplant. After chopping is finished, he leans heavily against the wall. It is a technique he developed while young to make his tallness somehow less intimidating when talking to people. I imagine him, adolescent and awkward, trying to make others around him comfortable. And then I watch him talk. Once a woman at a workshop told me my skin looks like the dark juice right after a berry has been plucked. They were not her words, I think she was quoting Maya Angelou, but I still found the way she said it beautiful enough to remember. Looking at his skin, which is two shades darker than mine, I wonder what she would think if she saw him. In my head I rap along to Tupac: *the darker the berry, the sweeter the juice.*

Standing by the wall, he begins telling me how a client of his had to send him some high Intel information in order to figure out the IT malfunction of the server. He knew the client was nervous to send the information because it included the budget of the company. He says, these American multinationals and NGOs hire a director who is a national and the person below them is always an American. But really it's only for the paperwork. The American gets a paid house, a car, benefits, and twenty thousand dollars a month. The national . . . *ha!* Peanuts. The national is never given such benefits. Such is the way of the world. Of our world. Or our Uganda at least.

I think of some friends of mine. How upset they get when they are passed over in their jobs for some white American who is significantly less intelligent, articulate and experienced. After-work beers consist of blasting stupid muzungus, ex-pats, and a government that would rather shit on its citizens than empower them. It upsets me too but I never know how to say it in a way that doesn't make me sound like a white liberal trying to be down with the cause. Moses continues telling me, you know, half these foreigners come into Africa with nothing of their own back home. I mean, why would someone who has it together in France come and work for a telecom company in Uganda? They come with their mediocrity and get the best-paying jobs. I nod my head and say, Amin had the right idea. He kicked the Indians out before and now they're all coming back with an economic vengeance. We should kick them out again. He looks at me. Baby, you're such a racist. I sigh, I'm not racist. I just think there should be a quota on the number of foreign investors in a country per national investors. If capitalism is going be around for a while, then at least let more nationals profit from the exploitation than foreigners. He cries, but that's worse! When your own people screw you over! I tell him, every suggestion will be worse. It is his turn to sigh, anyway these foreigners would not have as much power if the president did not sell off every piece of national land like this country is his personal yard sale . . . and people are not demanding enough from the government. Complacency will always beget complacency. It's not just civic education, our whole education system needs to be revamped! I look at him and say, hmm. Yeah babe, Biko called, he wants his philosophy back. Again he laughs that deep laugh of his as I continue, but I still say kick the Indians out. He smiles, such a racist! A racist and an imperialist, the perfect match. While talking, we have managed to prepare something colourful. But it turns out too exotic to eat more than three bites. We drink the remaining wine and leave the food for his brother.

The following weekend I receive an invitation for a variety show hosted at the U.S. Ambassador's house. I

RSVP as a guest. The night of the show I show up by myself but once inside I realise I know many people in attendance. The event is taking place on the front lawn and I straight away notice two fully-stocked bars at either side of the garden. Waiters are moving about serving guests chicken skewers and chickpea samosas. The garden tent has a crystal chandelier that is so extravagant you can't help but stare at it even when you are trying to avoid it. Someone next to me says in baffled amusement, I have never in my life seen a crystal chandelier in a garden tent. I think, ditto.

While the ambassador is delivering his speech about the bridging of cultures, the diversity in multiculturalism and democracy, I lean toward a tall woman I have seen at other art shows, and I say, but we should not be fooled. A variety show tonight but by tomorrow morning he'll be back in the president's office forcing him to sign yet another ridiculous interest-based loan and non-tariffed import agreement. She looks at me, then turns away and walks to join a group of laughing white men. I continue drinking my wine, and after my fourth glass, I text Moses: *The ambassador's house is bigger than the town of Ttula. Life is not fair.* He texts me back: *My car is bigger than Ttula!* And a few minutes later he sends another text: *Life is fair. Taxes are not.*

Later that night, tipsy at his place, I revel in his tight grip as we move from staircase to bedroom. In the middle of making love, his phone rings. Rule two: when making sexy-time, phones are supposed to be off and most definitely are not to be answered. But it is three o' clock in the morning and I am wondering who aside from a family member reporting death could be calling him at such a time. Because I am on top, I see the flashing vibrating phone on the drawer next to the bed. The letter T flashes and I suddenly find myself un-aroused. Moses looks at me. Why the hell would someone call me three o' clock in the morning? I look him in the eye, I don't know—it's probably important. Pick it up. He shakes his head no. They can call again tomorrow. By this time I am climbing off him. Baby, come back, he pleads. Where are you going?

I sit on the toilet and wonder what the hell I have gotten myself into. Moses is married. He has never lied about it. In fact, he told me on our third date. That he had been separated for one and a half years but that according to God and his missionary mother he was still a married man. Kids? I had asked him. No, he'd said, we have no children together. Business investments? He laughed. I love the way you don't fear asking such questions. No, we had no business investments together. No property owned together. None of that! At which I'd asked the obvious, so why aren't you divorced? Too painful, he had responded. She is drama. Was when we dated, was when we were married, is while we're separated. But there is nothing there. I'm just waiting for the two years legal separation and then I divorce her. And in that moment of feminine yearning, I believed him.

T called once a week. If anyone else called—a potential client, his lawyer, or even his sister—Moses never left the room. But when T called, he always ignored the phone. He never told me who T was and I never asked.

I grew up watching my mother go through my dad's pockets. I would watch her cry as she found numbers and love notes. I had promised myself, at ten years old, that that would never be me. That I would never run around crying after men who couldn't value me outside good sex and delicious meals. And here I was, seated in the bathroom at three o'clock in the morning because I knew T was his wife. Babe, I hear his voice outside the door, you've been in there for a while. I miss you. You left me hanging. Come back to bed. I shake my head and respond, I'll be right there.

I hear his footsteps receding. Sure and steady steps, the kind that know where they are going. Mine? Heavy feet stuck to the floor. I somehow muster the strength to walk out of the bathroom and crawl back into bed. With my back turned to him, I curl into myself. Wrapping his arms around me, he begins kissing the nape of my neck. Not right now, I say into the pillow, my voice muffled but still audible. That's alright, baby, that's alright, he purrs in my ear.

My mother calls me in the morning to tell me she has not received the email I sent her the night before. Our conversation is brief as it is one in the morning her time and she is going to bed. Right before she says bye, I say, Mama, let me ask you, what is better to use when you're with someone, the head or the heart? She pauses before saying, I didn't realize you were seeing anyone, Solo. I'm not, I'm not, I say quickly. Just asking . . . the head or the heart? She pauses again. Solome. I'm surprised you have to ask. Think of everything we've been through. Remember when we were in the storm, the belly of the beast I guess you can call it? We went through the tough times together, and you know better than I do that the head is what led us to better places. If I followed my heart, we would not be where we are. It is always the head, Solo. Always the head.

PEOPLE OF THE VALLEY

Makhosazana Xaba

This is *Talk to Thuli at Twelve.* Sanibonani Sanibonani, you people of the valley. Welcome to your day's favourite programme, *Talk to Thuli at Twelve.* This is your loyal Vukavuka Community Radio station, 101 FM. Kusinwa kudedelwana bakithi. Out goes Bheki Mavuso, in comes Thulisile Thabethe. Out goes one-way traffic, in comes two-way traffic. Out goes information, in comes conversation. I'm your host at twelve, and for the next hour you and I mlaleli will ta-a-a-alk. If you're tuning in for the first time, welcome dear listener. During the next hour all we do is ta-a-a-alk. We talk about any topic at all as long as it affects residents of the valley, us. Unfortunately today, I say unfortunately, the topic for today was chosen by the universe and not by you people of the valley. I'm sure you all agree with me that today we have no choice but to talk about the news that broke this morning at about 6am. Sad news though it is, it's our news, our community, our issue, therefore for us to understand and solve or simply talk about.

Now if you have not yet heard the news, let me break it to you gently. Those of you who are regular listeners know that I try to walk every morning. This morning as I was getting ready to say goodbye to my mother and walk out of the house, the news broke. My mother leaves the house promptly at 6.30am so we always say our goodbyes when I leave for my walk at six. When I get back to the house, it's just her chickens, my goats and myself. I was tying my laces when I heard it.

Last night apparently the police arrested Matron Langa. I don't think there's anyone in the valley who doesn't know Matron Langa. She came to the valley fifteen years ago and has done amazing work at Philani Community Health Centre, a 24-hour clinic, first of its kind in the whole region. Children who were born when she first came are now going to high school. She delivered many of them, many of us, I should say. I myself was only ten years old when she first came to the valley. Today I speak to you as a radio talk show host. Matron Langa had the vision that led to the renovation, upgrading and extension of Philani Clinic. She knew how to talk *to* government people. She knew how to talk *for* her people. She was tireless in her efforts. She came from the other side of the mountain but once she was in the valley, she became one of us, beautiful people of the valley. Some people actually say that without her, we would still have a small clinic that only opens during the day. The staff has increased from four to twenty. There is a three-bed maternity ward and a casualty unit that opens all night. We even have an ambulance now that we share with people of the Njoko clan on the other side of the mountain.

The lines are buzzing already, but let me first finish the story. Allegedly, someone tipped off the police and they went and raided Matron Langa's home. They found a freezer full of women's placentas. Yes, the police had the organs tested and it's been confirmed they are placentas, most of them full-term ones. For those young people who have no idea what a placenta is, let me explain it to you as it was explained to me. When a baby grows in its mother womb, it connects with its mother through the umbilical cord, *inkaba* in isiZulu. That is what midwives cut soon after the baby has come out. Now that cord is the extension of the placenta, a flat mass of tissue that looks a bit like the liver *isibindi*, but not smooth like the liver. It's that organ that helps to attach the baby to the inside of its mother's womb. With a normal birth, this placenta comes out of the woman soon after the baby has come out. Now I am told midwives have a system for throwing this thing away. Apparently they are required by law to throw this away, dispose of it. But apparently in this case Matron Langa took these placentas home and put them in her freezer. Staff at Philani are in shock. Some say it cannot be true. No one knows why. She is in police custody as we speak, and I have confirmed this information. I spoke to the station commander. Matron says she is not saying a thing until her lawyer arrives.

Now, people of the valley what do you have to say to this? Shocking news indeed. Call me on the number that you now know so well, TTTAT for *Talk to Thuli at Twelve,* let's hear your say. Yes, the lines have been buzzing, so I won't waste time. Yes, welcome Ma Duma.

Thuli Mtanami, nguwelowo?

Yes, Ma Duma,yimi.

Listen here my child, I am your grandmother and you know I listen to you every day, I have been sitting here waiting for you to come on my radio. Was it last year when I called and said ubuthakathi busabaphethe abantu abamnyama? Remember? This is simple and straightforward. Matron Langa is a witch. Period. Why do you think she left her village? She never visits her people, do you know that?

No MaDuma, but how do you know that she never goes home?

Thuli, my grandparents okhokho bokhokho ungizwa kahle, they were born here eVukavuka. When Vukavuka was a peaceful valley. We who have been here through our ancestors from the beginning of time know everything about everybody in this valley. Even this radio station of yours, we know all about it.

Thank you, Ma Duma. Let's hear what others have to say on this matter. Ma Duma has raised a few issues. If you've just tuned in, I am Thulisile Thabethe on your special talk show *Talk to Thuli at Twelve*, where we discuss issues affecting our community. And this is your favourite radio station, Vukavuka Community Radio. Next caller, yes BL, go ahead.

Thuli, I say this is a shame, this is a shame that has befallen our community and we need to do something about it. I'm not sure what, but this is a bad sign. When respectable people of the community start doing such horrible things it means one and one thing only, konakele, konakele, Thuli, bye that's all I wanted to say.

Hmm thank you, BL. People of the valley, do you agree with BL when he says, I think he was saying, that this incident is a sign that something bigger is wrong, this incident is – just as we say in the valley – the tip of the mountain?

Welcome to Vukavuka Community Radio, our next caller is Mxo, yes, Mxo. Talk to Thuli.

Hellow Thuli, thanks for taking my call. I am calling from the primary school eVulamehlo. I teach Grade Three and as I speak to you my children have left the school. At about ten a woman came to fetch all the children who were born at Philani. She says she wants the police to make Matron Langa identify their placentas.

What? Are you serious?

I am dead serious Thuli, half the pupils in my class have left and some of the other teachers have also lost pupils. Mrs Khanya our principal in fact asked me to call your show so you can appeal to the community to be calm about this situation. She is trying to manage the situation as best as she can. I tell you Thuli, it's chaos here. Some parents have started coming individually to take their children.

Identifying placentas to what end? What are they saying this will achieve?

Thuli, I also don't understand it very well, I've just been told that it's important. I think it's got to do with ancestors. Please Thuli, talk to the community. We need calm all round.

Now whoever thought that frozen placentas could create such panic! I can't believe this! Mxo, thanks for your call. We *are* talking and talking is one way of dealing with the problem. The lines have not stopped buzzing. Talk to me, our next caller is Masande.
Yes, Masande.

Yebo Thuli. Nginga khuluma ngolwakithi?

Khululeka Masande, khululeka here on Vukavuka Community Radio sikhuluma zonke izilimi. Lithini-ke elakho Masande?

Thuli, ngivumelana nalo othi konakele esigodini sakwethu. Kwazi bani ukuthi wawuqala nini lomkhuba uMatronLanga? Kwazi bani ukuthi zingaki izibeletho zabafazi bawo wonke amathafa lawa eziphelele efrijini yakwakhe?Elami nje lithi akekho umuntu ongenza into enje engaguli, UMatron Langa uyagula, ugula ngekhanda? Sithi sinomhlengikazi nje kanti nguye qobo ogulayo. Ngiyaphela lapho Thuli.

Wow, thanks Masande. Now that's an interesting perspective. No one has said this so far. Masande says only a mentally sick person can do what Matron Langa allegedly did. But Masande also raises other questions. She wants to know how many placentas are in that freezer. She wants to know when Matron Langa started doing this. Well, she makes me think: is the freezer full of placentas only or are there other goodies in there? When I spoke to the station commander, he said they suspected by the way the freezer was packed that it was all placentas, but he had no clue as to how many there were and refused to even estimate. I believe they are waiting for the freezer to defrost completely before a forensics expert can confirm what all the goodies are. They are expecting one from the city by three this afternoon.

I'm your talk show host Thulisile Thabethe, and we are discussing the shocking news of Matron Langa's arrest. Next caller, Njenje, is that Njenje?

Yebo Thuli. Uyabona Thuli, abathiu Matron uyahlanya nami ngiyabavuna. The bigger question is how can we, all of us, have been fooled by this person who came from the other side of the mountain, made herself comfortable among us because we could not do things for ourselves, and now she has poisoned the whole valley?

Poisoned? What do you mean Bab'uNjenje?

Thuli ngithi isihlava sohlanya uMatron Langa, uyasazi isihlava? Before we know it the whole community will be rotten, just like her. A Matron who poses as a healer ends up poisoning the community what do you call that, hhe?

People of the valley, please, I know this is shocking for all of us, but let's try and come up with solutions not accusations! Let's ask questions if we must, but questions that will help lead us to answers. Calling Matron Langa names is not going to deal with our situation. Now, if someone – a nurse, or a doctor on duty, a midwife, anyone who really knows from Philani Community Health Centre is listening, please call Vukavuka Community Radio Station. I would like to know the step-by-step process that midwives and doctors are expected to follow when disposing of the placenta. Why do I want to know this? I think, well I hope, that an informed answer to this question will help us understand even in a small way why Matron did what she did. Maybe there is a simple answer. Maybe placentas can only be disposed of in bulk, for cost-effectiveness. We simply don't know at this stage. Next caller on the line, Libuyile. Talk to me Libuyile, you are calling from the secondary school Qhubekani.

Yes Sis Thuli. As you know I'm like a regular caller on your cool show. I'm like responsible for our newsletter Vukavuka Valley Voice. *Needless to say Sis Thuli, our school is also like in major like shock, but I'm like calling to tell you what my fellow students have decided to do. When you asked for solutions I thought I should like holla at ya, you know like tell you what we're doing.*

Go ahead Libuyile, that's so good to hear.

But before I go into that and I know you just said we need to stop with the accusing and find a solution but I like really need to put this out there. Sis Thuli, don't you think it's like totally and utterly gross when you think about where she was keeping these things. I mean, I know like anywhere else and they would have gone rotten and smelled horrible but I mean this was her like freezer where she kept her food, her food Sis Thuli. Can you imagine like every night going into your freezer and deciding to like take out your chicken breasts to defrost and having to like move aside thousands of women's bodily organs? Old bodily organs, I might add!

I hardly think it was anywhere near a thousand, Libuyile.

Ok, so maybe I'm exaggerating a little but still, iyuuuu! Back to your solution, Libuyile. Let's hear it.

Ok, ok Sis Thuli, the editorial team. We like held an emergency meeting, you know, to talk about this issue, neh. And our focus was what can we like contribute, so we like thought statistics would be cool. So like besides the regular reporting and releasing a special issue on this alone we're going to do a kinda survey, you know, research.

Hmm, I like the sound of that Libuyile, you go girl. Tell us more about your research, but please try and speed up or we will be running out of time.

Yes Sis Thuli. Well the idea isn't fine-tuned yet but we were thinking we could do something like going to Philani and asking them like exactly how many kids were delivered by this matron and who they are, neh. When I think about it, any of my Grade Eight and Nine friends (I say Eight and Nine coz we're only a high school, remember) could have been delivered by this woman and like had their placentas stuffed in a freezer. I mean, what's with that? Anyhoo, moving on. Then neh, we could go to those kids and interview them. Ask them questions like how they feel about their placenta being in like a freezer for so long. And whether they're not like totally grossed out. Now we're like expecting the majority of these guys and gals to be under fifteen, like you said. So when we see the completely miffed looks on their faces the next question will obviously be like whether they even know what a placenta is and whether they care.

I like that, Libuyile. I like it very much. But please, please, call her Matron Langa. She is not "this woman," she continues to be Matron Langa. We prefer some respect on this radio station.

My bad Sis Thuli, I'm just really peeved by this whole thing, so is the whole committee.

That's all right Libuyile, but my question to you is how's that gonna help the police investigation, the people of the valley, or even Matron for that matter?

Well Sis Thuli, as said earlier the idea is not like exactly fine-tuned yet, neh, mara we're getting there. And we're determined to help in some way. People of the valley need to know that kids have brains and can make a major diff if you let us.

So tell me Libuyile, does your committee have money to do this research?

Hhayi six no nine, seven nes'bhamu Sis Thuli, we'll find a way.

There you have it people of the valley, our young people also want to have their say. They want to make a difference. Libuyile, I wish you and your team all the best. Come back and talk to us at *Talk to Thuli at Twelve* once your research is on the go.

Ngiyabonga Sis Thuli, bye. Thanks for listening, my chomies and editorial team will be so like excited.

Next caller, you're welcome Mrs Khuzwayo. This has to be such an interesting topic for people of the valley. The callers are so passionate today. Mrs Khuzwayo, you're on air.

Thank you, Thulisile. I want to ask the people of the valley two questions. One: how different is this Matron Langa story from the thousands of stories of rape of girls and women we hear about all over the country? Two: how different is Matron Langa's story from the deputy president's story of corruption and fraud? I say these cases are not different.

You will have to say more there, Mrs Khuzwayo.

Thuli, it's logic, Matron Langa is taking away women and children's dignity, in this case mere newborns. Isn't this what rapists do? Matron Langa is using her power to fool the people just like the deputy president.

Mrs Khuzwayo, the deputy president still has to go to court. He has not, I repeat, not been found guilty yet.

OK Thuli I get you, my apologies. Let me just say Matron Langa is just like all other people who are in power, in high positions all over the country, who fool the common people. They pretend to be someone they are not. Matron Langa has fooled us all. We thought we had an angel of a matron, now we know she is the devil herself.

But Mrs Khuzwayo, she has not been found guilty yet.

Point is Thuli, someone blew the whistle on her. Someone knew something we didn't know. I bet you it's one of her colleagues. Me, I don't even want to know the disposal procedure, I just know that if there's someone who blew the whistle, then Matron Langa is not following the procedure. They knew something was freezing unprocedurally, illegally in Matron's freezer, and they told the police. Everyone working at Philani has to talk. It's time to tell the truth now.

Mrs Khuzwayo…

I bet you Thuli ngifung' aMaNgidi ephelele, a lot more people know something about this but one person was brave enough to tell.

Yes Mrs Khuzwayo, can you please…

And, Thuli, and, I'm about to finish, my theory is that she was selling these placentas to someone somewhere somehow. I mean, why else would she keep so many? She is getting rich on women's dignity and individual pride. How can anyone born in Vukavuka during the She-devil matron's time say where their umbilical cord is buried? That's us Thuli, that's just who we are as a people.

Mrs Khuzwayo –

No, honestly Thuli, everyone wants to be able to say with pride where their umbilical cord was buried. Don't you?

Mrs Khuzwayo, sorry, I am going to have to cut you off. The lines are buzzing, many people need to talk. We get your point about dignity but to call Mrs Langa a she-devil is uncalled for. Not on this radio station, please. Our next caller, yes, welcome to *Talk to Thuli at Twelve.* Jongiwe, you are next, talk to me.

Molweni, thanks Thuli, sana I am very, very surprised that so many callers are talking like this. The only person that has made sense to me so far is Mrs Khuzwayo. I think she is right about something, what if Matron Langa is in business, iphi ingxaki apho? Thuli sana, how many times have you yourself said on this radio station that women must stop complaining and start acting. Matron Langa saw an economic opportunity and acted. There's only one reason to keep so many of the placentas, to sell, you know sana, make money.

Jongiwe, so you are saying the matron should be left alone because we all have the constitutional right to make money anyway we like?

Thulisana, let me ask you and your listeners a question, people throw away plastic bags right? Others collect these, cut them up and make items from them, and sell those items, you know floor mats, place mats, hats, right? Others collect them and create artistic pieces from plastic, right? They make money from what others consider waste. Now, who says it's illegal to use human waste in this case, placentas? Tell me Thuli, since when is that illegal?

I must say that's an interesting and fresh take on this issue. Thanks, Jongiwe. Listeners, if you have just tuned in, this is your favourite midday programme *Talk to Thuli at Twelve* on 101 FM. Jongiwe asked a pertinent question: what is wrong with Matron Langa using this economic opportunity, human waste? Our next caller is Sembathiseni, you are calling from the Gwinyama the General Dealers, right?

Yes Thuli. As someone from the shop I also agree with the last caller, what's her name?

Jongiwe. Her name is Jongiwe. Please go on.

Yes, Jongiwe. I actually take my hat off for Matron Langa. To me she is a hero of which I support. First she came to our Valley and changed things the way we had never imagined, aneh? Mosdan that's what the new South Africa is all about, neh, of which it's working for our khawntry. That's all I wanted to say.

Thank you Sembathiseni, brief and to the point, let's build the economy for the country. Next caller, yes Prettyboy. Did you say your name is Prettyboy?

Yes Thuli, it's just a nickname you know mos. Me, I want to argue a new point. If people are now agreeing that Matron was in business, who, tell me who, would want to buy placentas? To do what with them? Thuli, when people make statements I think they need to support them. Who would buy placentas, what are they useful for?

Prettyboy, pretty point. I take your point eh. Mrs Khuzwayo and Jongiwe, if you are still listening please call the station back. I want to know what you think of Prettyboy's challenge. It's a simple point. If Matron Langa is trading in human organs, who might she be selling them to, in other words what's their value? If you've just tuned in, this is *Talk to Thuli at Twelve,* 101FM. Next caller, you're on air Makwenzeke.

Thank you for taking my call, Thuli. I have been listening now for a long, long time. I think everyone is missing a very significant angle. I think it's sad that the people of the valley, my people, are so quick to jump to conclusions.

Makwenzeke, I have to interrupt you there, please won't you come to the point. What's your significant angle?

My angle, Thuli, is the most simple one, most sensible one, most matter-of-fact and practical one. Research. Thuli, a place as big as Philani Community Health Centre is an ideal place for researchers to do their work, right? And we live in a unique geographical area of KZN province. I want to believe that there are peculiarities that are found only in our area that call for research. Agree?

I hear you. Proceed.

Matron Langa is the most senior person at this health centre, right?

Ja-ja.

So, who would be taking responsibility for research samples? Mrs Langa of course, right?

Now I think you have an interesting new angle there, Makwenzeke. Are you a health professional yourself?

No, I was just working for six months for a pharmaceutical company, and I know that they use clinics and hospitals a lot for information. They collect samples from large clinics and hospitals and use them to find answers to research questions.

Interesting indeed! Would you have any ideas of what answers could be sought from placentas?"

No Thuli, I don't know, but if I were to hazard a guess I would say it has to do with maybe genetic research, you know this DNA stuff everyone talks about. A placenta is located in a key position between the mother and her baby, so I think, I said I think, that's the kind of research they, someone, some pharmaceutical company may be doing.

Thank you Makwenzeke. A new angle indeed. The question remains though, supposing, just supposing that Makwenzeke is right, wouldn't the rest of the staff at Philani know about this ongoing research? Why would anyone tell on the Matron if she was doing what the last caller suggests? You are listening to *Talk to Thuli at Twelve*,101 FM. Next caller, you're on air.

Thuli! Is that Thuli?

Yes caller, you are on air. Talk to me.

Can you hear me there?

Yes I said you are on air already. Talk to me.

Thuli! Is this the radio?

Bad, bad line I'm afraid I'm gonna have to cut you there. We have time for a few more calls. Mrs Mthethwa, you are next, please talk to me.

Thuli you know me, me I think there's a lot of truth in what the early, early callers were saying. You see I think people of the valley are losing their traditions. You know before these hospitals and clinics arrived, people had enormous respect for the placenta. They buried it ceremonially you know, there used to be a special ritual for burying the placenta.

Tell us what it was, please, Mrs Mthethwa.

Sorry Thuli even I don't know it, but my grandmother used to tell me that the reason so many people leave their homes and never return, some never even have the desire to return, is because they were never rooted properly in the soil.

People of the valley, if anyone knows the rituals of burying the placenta, please, please, please, give us a call before this show ends, and that's pretty soon. Now, can I ask every single caller waiting to speak to please keep it short. The lines have not stopped, everyone in the valley has something to say. So please be brief and come with a new angle. Next, Baba Mbonambi, you're on air.

Thuli, thank you for the time. You were still in napkins when Matron Langa arrived here. We used to listen to uKhozi radio. Your station is just three years old.

Baba Mbonambi we all know that, your point please.

My point is simple: people who are old enough still remember that this Matron Langa, when she came here, she came under a cloud.

Meaning?

Meaning two things, one: people said she is a Kwerekwere from Mozambique, that she changed her name and chose an easy one that she could pronounce. Two: people said, note I say people said, she had killed her husband in Mozambique. That's all I wanted to remind you young ones.

Wow, Baba Mbonambi. I don't know if I want to go there. Listeners, people of the valley, I feel I don't know what I feel. Any comments on what Baba Mbonambi has just said, eh? This is *Talk to Thuli at Twelve* on your one and only community radio station, the station for the people. Next caller on the line, Singabakho. Singabakho, I've always loved that name. Talk to me. Talk to us, Singabakho.

Firstly Thuli Mr Mbonambi is right about those rumours. They did circulate when she first arrived here. But hey, I also killed my husband after twenty years of violent abuse and numerous rapes that I reported to the police and the community over the years. That's why I won my case in court. I came to this valley to escape my community down there in the south coast. Some of them wanted me to go to jail. But that's not my point. My point is this: me, I think the other nurses at Philani Community Health Centre should come on radio and clarify things for us. There's far too many questions around this, we need clarity and facts before we can discuss. That's my request.

Great points there, Singabakho. Wow, thanks for sharing that personal story as well, Ma. Moving. Touching. In fact, I think we need to do a show, another show, on that topic, women who murder their husbands. Wheh! Very, very, moving! I agree and appeal to staff members at the Philani Health Centre to please call the station and give us their perspectives on this issue. I asked for this earlier, listeners want it as well. Principal MaNkosi on the line. Yes Madam Principal, you are on air.

Thuli, as you know I am the principal and owner of the creche, I am surprised that no one is talking about Matron Langa's human rights. I want to make one point, let's hear from a lawyer what rights Matron Langa has under such circumstances. First and foremost, what has she been charged with? What is the charge? Do you know if I am keeping dead rats in my freezer, do the police have the right to come and take me to the police station? For what, hhe? Thank you.

Good point principal, it reminds me that in fact my producer has been trying to get hold of Advocate Nomali Mnikathi, who is always ready to advise us on legal matters. She is in court and might call in soon. So, yes, we are going to go there. Next caller, Nomazizi. Nomazizi, talk to me.

Ja, thanks. I have this idea that sort of builds on that one by that caller who spoke about research. I would like to know what else is kept in freezers by all the nurses who work at Philani Health Centre. I have also heard many stories about people trading in human organs and researchers acquiring body parts without permission. If the police were to go and check all the freezers of the staff who live in that boarding house – how many are they, ten? – who knows what they would find? That's all I wanted to say, Thuli.

To the point, Nomazizi! I am going straight to the police station at the end of this show, by the way. Next caller, Phathizwe.

Me, I think we are being called upon to pray. We need to pray hard for this community. The primary school has been closed now. Children have all left, the gates are locked. And there is a long queue of people outside the PCHC gate and the security people are stopping people from jumping over the fence. I live right next to the school, and the PCHC is walking distance from there, I have just come from there. So, me, I just wanted to suggest Thuli that you close this show with a prayer. God bless you and the people of this valley. Amen.

Phathizwe, Amen there. We have time for the last two callers. To the point, please. Thathiwe, you're on.

I just wanted to say I agree with Phathizwe, but I think people should also pray for Matron Langa. But my point is simple, please warn the community Thuli, no one should be attacked during this whole confusion. No one! That's all, thank you.

Brief and the point! I couldn't agree with you more there, Thathiwe. Last and final caller, Njengelanga, you're our last caller on *Talk to Thuli at Twelve.* Let's hear your point. Njengelanga.

Thuli, that caller who told us she killed her husband, wow, what courage! I am curious as well about the rumours about Matron Langa. She has no children, no known relatives, we and when I say we, I mean us young people, mostly we just love her because we have known her all our lives. She just seems to have been here all the time, like the river and the mountain. So I wanted to suggest, Thuli, that when this whole fracas is over, invite her to the show. We love her, we will listen. Thanks, that's all I wanted to say.

People of the valley, this ends our show for today. This show will go down in history as the show during which phones rang non-stop from the first minute at twelve to this very last minute. My producer Musawenkosi is sweating. His fingers are numb from pressing the buttons. Thanks, Musa. To the rest of the technical team: Ndawoyethu, Dedanimabhunu, Velemazweni and Tholakele, as always: many thanks!

Wow, I have to breathe. I cannot even begin to summarise the main points of our show today. What a pity no one called from the clinic. It would have been great to get a perspective from someone working there. But we get it people of the valley, don't we? And we empathise. I imagine the clinic is pretty hectic as we speak. I'll make sure we speak to someone from the clinic tomorrow.

One more promise: I'll be back with you tomorrow at *Talk to Thuli at Twelve.* Nisalekahle. Nisalekahle, you people of the valley. This is your loyal Vukavuka Community Radio station, find us on 101 FM. I am Thulisile Thabethe at *Talk to Thuli at Twelve* signing off. Ngangezwe Ngubane coming up next. It's one o'clock.

People of the Valley was first published in 'Running and Other Stories' by Makhosazana Xaba, (Modjaji Books 2013)

ALLETJIE EVERYTHING

Karen Jennings

Alletjie came around the corner of the cottage with a bucket in either hand. The rain beat down on her and made ringing sounds as it hit the metal pails. Nearby, patches of wild shrubs that the goats hadn't yet touched lay flattened by the downpour. Orange earth splashed up against the hem of her dress and clung to her work shoes. An inheritance from her brother, they were too large and had been stuffed with newspaper to prevent them slipping from her feet. The handle of one of the buckets squealed in the rain and chickens hiding in their coops clucked angrily at the sound. From beneath a low thorn tree to the right of the yard, the dog, wet and orange with mud, bounded towards her, pushing his head into the pails in search of food. She kicked him away, swearing, 'You bleddy mutt.' Had her hands not been occupied she would have reached into the pocket of her six-days-a-week dress for the pebbles that she kept there and chased the creature from the yard. Instead, she kicked it again and walked on, scowling.

Her face had been darkened over the years by labour, and the whites of her narrow eyes had yellowed with time, her eyebrows balding as grey flecked the hair under her doek. She lived with her husband, Jan Bakker, and her brother, Solly, who they had taken in. Seventeen years before, a mining accident had brought a rock down on his leg. In the dark underground, by means of headlamps and shoving, his fellow miners determined the rock immovable. Using a saw from a farmer's tool-shed, they amputated the leg at the thigh. There had been no anaesthetic. Small rocks had been loosened by the screams he managed before passing out. By morning the following day he was delirious. The leg that he no longer had spoke to him. It told him what it was like to live under a rock, abandoned. How spiders crawled over the toes, lizards licked the bloodied shreds. Solly begged his family for the leg to be returned to him. To have the thing brought home, as though it were a baby he had thought to give up, but had changed his mind about. He cried; a mother without her infant. The real hurt came later. When he had become aware that those things which in the past had moved in step with him had all retreated. In one day he had lost a job, the ordinariness of movement, and all the world. Something as familiar as a trip to the toilet had become irrevocably distant. At first the number of things that had retreated were too numerous to contemplate and he lay bed-ridden for months in self-pity. But with time he had taken up the wooden crutches he had been given, and he walked with them the short distances that were allowed a man with one leg living in the wilderness.

The three of them lived on the slopes of an abandoned copper mine. Solly sat in the yard, keeping mainly silent in depression as he collected his memories and stroked the yellow dog's head. Bakker often lounged in the dirt close by, or walked the rocky outcrop, surveying his property and the town's houses a few kilometres away. On the distant road cars passed which Solly might count or ignore as he pleased. Sometimes strangers followed the dirt road to the cottage, having seen the old stone mine bins built in the 1880s by the hands of Cornish miners. Then Solly would call to Bakker, who guarded the mine as though it were his own land. 'Tourists,' he would shout, his voice echoing through the silent wasteland.

For a small fee Bakker would show them the bins, walk them up and down the mine heaps at a pace remarkable in a man of his age. He showed them the caverns and cavities he had worked in his youth and pointed out the dangers of falling into these pits. 'Birds have flown in and never found their way out. And don't never leave the gate open. The goats will wander over and fall in and break their legs. Look here,' he said, dropping a pebble into a pit. It caused a small rockslide, the numbers of pebbles increasing as they made their way downwards. 'See how the rocks will fall on it. Here we own no gun to shoot the animals if they fall in. They will take a long time to die, in pain with broken legs, or their stomachs crushed by falling rocks. Have you ever heard a goat scream?' He tried to mimic the sound, watching as the visitors flinched away. 'And how will we live without our goats? We are poor. Very poor,' he would repeat, encouraging an extra tip from their pockets for his time.

Alletjie walked into the cottage that was thick with the dampness of a green wood fire. 'Coffee's finished,' Bakker said as she entered. He was sitting on a three-legged stool, chewing the end of a pipe he had never smoked. His stomach rested on his knees, his beard dragged on his chest. 'And the sugar.'

'You didn't think to buy any when you were in town this morning?'

'With what money?'

'The disability money for Solly. Isn't that what you went to the post office to get? Where's it now?'

Bakker shrugged his heavy shoulders. 'Finished.'

She put the pails down near the kitchen table and turned towards him, scowling through the smoke. 'Finished? How? On drink, you skelm. You steal money from your own family for dop, like a criminal!'

Again he shrugged his shoulders.

In the neighbouring room, Solly lay on the mattress that was his bed. He had been lying there all afternoon, listening to the rain on the metal roof of the cottage. He heard the raised voice of his sister, Bakker's answering silence, and he rolled over, reaching for the emptiness where his leg had once been. He took a pillow and used it to fill the space left open by its absence. He wondered whether anyone would come in and help him up. He could not do it on his own.

#

The rain had continued steadily, until the grey sky had darkened into a wet night. Alletjie stood in the open doorway, frowning into the weather. 'It's bad, this wind,' she said to herself. On the table she had set the washed bowls and spoons from their dinner. Soup again; the eighth day in a row with nothing to eat but soup. No wonder her breasts sagged and her legs felt weak as she walked the wild trails of their property. Fifty-two years old and ready for the grave. She remained in the doorway for some time, hesitating, hearing through the storm the sound of something clanging. Not the sound of a leaky ceiling dripping water into metal pails. Not Solly crutching his way across the cold stone floor towards his seat beside the fire. She walked a few paces out into the yard in order to hear better. A chicken clucked.

'Be quiet you,' she muttered. Damn chickens. And damn the rain too. Damn this patch of the world where it was always too hot, too cold, too dry, too wet. Always goats and chickens, goats and chickens. She'd eaten more of them in her life than she could count. Her daddy a miner, her brother a miner, her cousins miners, all ruined by that underground life. And then her husband also a miner when she had married him, aged fifteen, knowing no better. Miners and farmers. What else was there for a man to be? Afterwards the mines had closed and no one could find work and he had made her move here to this hovel on the back of the old mine, as though he hadn't been able to let the damned place go. Here where there was nothing, just piles of rock and green stone and orange dirt that yielded nothing. Living on the old goats and chickens and a disability grant that was never enough.

And Bakker wasn't popular. He fought. He knew better than anyone else. He couldn't take orders. No one would employ him. Not twice, not even once. No one would lend him money. He drank too much. But all three of them did. Their bottles hidden, their breaths and flushed faces a silent code of unity. 'And why not?' she thought. Why shouldn't she have a little something from time to time, out here on this godforsaken mine. She did her work, didn't she? She didn't get out of hand like some people did. So why not have a little something, just a little something to keep her going out here. Mechanically she put her hands in her pockets, feeling for the pebbles that lived there. They were heavy in her hand and gave her some comfort.

But the rain was falling harder now, the wind more fierce, and still she could hear the clanging from some unidentified source. She craned her neck out into the dark wet night. All the world beyond the yard was hidden from her. But then, as though she had known it all along, she recognised the sound. It was the gate, the gate leading to the mine. It had come loose in the wind and was slamming in and out.

'Bakker, the gate!'

His voice was muffled, lazy, 'I'm busy, woman. Do it yourself or did God not give you two arms and two legs?'

'Bleddy good-for-nothing,' she muttered. Yet she hurried towards the gate anyway, pulling her doek down over her forehead, her lips sputtering. In her haste, the mud loosened under Alletjie's shoes, sending her downwards, her back and sides covered. That was enough. She needed no more, just that, and she rose slowly, moving now towards the right, towards the shelter where the goats rested at night, untethered. There they all were. Asleep despite the storm. From her pocket she lifted the stones, flinging them at snouts and rumps in an effort to drive them towards the open gate.

'Go!' she hissed at them. 'Make yourselves useful.'

They ran wildly, bleating, into the dark.

Now it was done and she paused a moment before turning around and forcing her tired legs to run up the muddy incline back to the cottage.

'Bakker! Bakker!' she called, tripping over the lintel, her feet lamed by mud.

He was still seated beside the fire, reaching across to take a brown bottle from Solly's outstretched hand.

'Woman, what is it?' he cried, slipping the bottle into the pocket of his jacket. 'You look like the ground took a shit on you. Ha-ha-ha, Solly, you see this?'

'The goats,' she wheezed at him. 'They got away. They're on the mine.'

His laughter stopped as he looked up at her. 'But how?'

'I don't know. The storm. The gate, I told you!'

'Well fetch them, dammit, instead of standing there dripping water everywhere and calling like a madwoman.' He reached for his pocket, readying to settle down again.

'Me? On that mine?' she said. 'You know I won't set foot on it. I won't. I won't do it. I swore to you and to God. Never again. The whole world knows I will not set foot near that place.'

'You and that mine,' he said, raising himself heavily and stumbling a bit. 'Alright, woman, bring me the torch, dammit.'

Jan Bakker walked outside. Around him the storm raged.

Inside the cottage, it was Alletjie's thoughts that drove her to stay where she was, her clothes caked, dripping on the stone floor. Yes, what he had said was true. She and that damned mine. Despite herself, she was tied to it, as she had been her whole life. Let it at last be of some use to her. She would not shout after him and call him back inside. Let it take another leg. An arm. Even a foot. Anything at all. Let it take something and in return she would gain for the three of them, but for herself mostly, the security of another disability grant.

Her breath came quickly as she thought of what she had in the world. A dress for weekdays, a dress for church. A brother worthless with depression. A husband who drank and slept and pined for the underground. The chickens, the goats, the labour was hers alone. She had no fear of work. She had known it long enough. But it had come between herself and life too often, this toiling, and this mine which ate parts of her family, with the result that it was always Alletjie that had to work harder. Where else had her name come from? *Alletjie wat alles doen. Alles.* Alletjie who does everything. Everything. Her hands shivered at her temples and she began to doubt the outcome of the plan. What if the mine was greedy? What if it wanted more than just a piece? What if Bakker was taken from her?

Beside the fire her brother sat between wake and sleep. The brandy that Bakker had snuck him had dulled his tongue and his half-closed eyes shone orange in the firelight. He saw his sister's agitation, felt it enter the room and sit amongst them like an uninvited guest.

'Is it still raining?' he asked.

'Ja.'

'He's not back yet?'

'Do you see him here?' she snapped.

She walked to the door, opening it fearfully. On

the lintel she craned forward, listening for cries for help. In her mind she rehearsed the scenes to come. She would hear him call. She would run to the farmhouse nearby. Twenty minutes to get there in this weather. Ten minutes back in the bakkie. Maybe fifteen if they stopped first to phone . . . phone who? There was no one near enough to phone who would be of any assistance. Should she be crying when she arrived? Or only after? And what about the saw? Would they think to bring it or would she have to tell them?

She shivered and stepped back inside the kitchen. But she stood a minute only contemplating the silence before she opened the door again, rabid with anticipation. She set her teeth. No call yet.

'Close the bleddy door,' her brother shouted. 'It's blowing the smoke in my eyes.'

She did and leaned violently against the doorframe.

'What's wrong with you? Why are you so agitated? Bakker's been on those mines more times than anyone else. They're his life, his blood. Stop fidgeting and sit down.'

'I am. I'm sitting.'

'Listen, while he's out . . . if you have booze, you must share,' he lectured. 'It will calm us down.'

'I have nothing. Where's yours?'

'Bakker took it with him. We'll have to wait for him.'

She grunted.

'He'll be back soon. I told you, those mines are like his blood,' her brother comforted her.

Only then did it occur to her. Something that she hadn't considered before. Worse than the mine taking all of him. It would take nothing. He would return from its holes and caverns unscathed. He wouldn't fall at all. It wasn't fair. The mine owed her this much. It owed her this future for herself.

She ran out into the dark, forgetting lamp and torch. She would go to the mine and she would find him. No one would guess. She would push him. She would find him and push him. Rocks would pin him down and no one would guess that she had been there. Or else, if they asked, she'd been reaching out to him, tried to save him.

Alletjie slid on her clay-clogged shoes towards the gate and began to hike up the dirt path towards the slopes of the mine. The rain had stopped and she could make out strange shapes hastening towards her. Ghosts. Ghosts of dead miners crawling towards her . . . but no, the shapes belonged to the goats she had driven away. They were making their way back to their shelter. And behind them, a hulking figure drove them onwards.

It was Jan Bakker returning.

THERE'S NOTHING TO SEE HERE

Davina Kawuma

I'm holding my breath because the conductor smells like the Irish I threw into the dustbin today. I can see my reflection in his specs whenever he turns around. He's the first conductor I've seen wearing specs. I didn't think conductors needed specs. All they ever do is pester people to give them money, anyway.

'Do you think I'm going to pass through the roof on my way out?' my mother sometimes asks the conductors, especially when they start pestering her soon after the taxi sets off. 'What if your taxi breaks down on the way? You'll get your money when I get to where I'm going.'

The conductors rarely say anything in return. When they do say something to her, though, it is often an apology. I find it surprising that even those people who don't know my mother as 'Mukyala Doctor Professor' are afraid of her.

Sitting like this, with my back against the driver's seat, is very uncomfortable. The heat from the engine is frying my buttocks, cross my heart, and my knees can't find enough space between mother's legs. Yet, if I don't sit here, on the kammeeme, the conductor will turn to my mother and say, 'Maama, kansuubire nti n'oy'ogenda kumusasulira ssente.' I don't like it when conductors refer to mother as 'Maama.'

'Obadde ki?' my mother often says. 'Nze ssente.'

My mother doesn't like the word vernacular—she says it sounds like the name of a disease, even though she speaks to me in it. She doesn't want me to grow up into one of our neighbour's children, who speak so much English that they probably cry in it. Not growing up into our neighbour's children is important in our home. That's why we know that the vernacular name for a loofah is kyangwe, and that both of them grow on a tree. Why we know that you get milk from the udder of a cow and not from the fridge. Why we know where the Old Taxi Park is. Why we wash our clothes and mop the house. Why, instead of threatening not to go to school when our mother can't drive us there, we walk to school. Why I sit on the kammeeme.

I don't always sit on the kammeeme, though. Sometimes, when I am not heavy, I sit on mother's lap. Today, though, her lap carries groceries from Owino market. She asks if I want a chocolate éclair. She smiles, too. Her smile starts at the corners of her mouth and ends at the hairline of her afro. I shake my head and look out the window. I don't want a chocolate éclair. I just want to be at home, right this moment. If not at home, then at school. If not at school, then in The Prevention.

I really miss The Prevention.

When Solomon was alive, we always called it by its full first name: THE PREVENTION OF VITAMIN A DEFICIENCY. (Its surname was A PROGRAM FUNDED BY UNICEF AND THE MINISTRY OF HEALTH.) After Solomon died, we shortened the name to The Prevention.

Some people say Solomon was killed because he refused to cooperate, that if he'd simply handed over the keys to The Prevention, without a fight, he'd probably still be alive. Some people say it wasn't The Prevention the thieves wanted, that they wanted Solomon's wristwatch. Some people say the thieves weren't after The Prevention or the wristwatch, and that the police found Solomon's body in The Prevention. His wristwatch was still on his wrist.

It was a Sunday, I think, when my father said, 'Solomon afudde. Bamusse.' The words seemed to be coming out of father's feet rather than his mouth. It occurred to me that I had never seen father's feet without socks. Father said Solomon was a good man and a hard-worker, and that he had a young family, and what would they do now that he was gone, and that this world is unfair.

After she heard the news, my mother sucked up all the air in the kitchen, covered her mouth, and turned her face to look up at something I could not see.

I went out to watch my brothers play dool and hit birds with butida, because I did not know what else I was supposed to do. The only other dead person I knew of at that time was my father's father, but I wasn't even born yet when he died. My mother must have said something about going to Solomon's funeral, and my father must have said something about paying for her transport. I can't remember if she went.

Father has a new car and a new driver, now. He is still anxious about driving in Kampala, even though it's been a while since he almost had that accident. Sometimes the new car breaks down on Bombo Road and I have to walk to school. I don't mind walking, but Mr. Tonda doesn't like it when any of us is late for morning assembly. He wants all of us to be on time to sing *Oh Uganda, may God uphold thee . . . we lay our future in thy hands . . . united free . . . for liberty together we . . . I can't remember the rest of it* in front of the library.

Sometimes, when I walk to school, I see The Prevention. It is still whiter than any PSV (Passenger Service Van, according to my mother, but Pakira Sasula Vaamu according to everyone in my class) and faster than THE FACULTY OF AGRICULTURE, MAKERERE UNIVERSITY, KAMPALA, UGANDA. I might be struggling up Wandegeya Road and The Prevention will turn off Lumumba Avenue. I might be hurrying past the World Vision offices and The Prevention will slow down beside me. Sometimes, Solomon gives me a lift. The seats in the back are hard, but at least I have my own seat. Sometimes, I have two or three seats. In The Prevention, I do not have to sit on the kammeeme.

Sometimes, Solomon smiles at me. Sometimes, he doesn't. Sometimes, he waves as he drives by. Sometimes, he doesn't.

One day, when I wanted to use the Nakasero Blood Bank shortcut, The Prevention appeared out of nowhere and parked itself next to the kiosk where Donald and I often buy glucose and musiba ttaayi. Solomon popped his head through the window and said I shouldn't go that way. I told him I was tired and didn't want to walk all the way round (which is what we'd all had to do since the road that branched off to the State House had been closed off). But Solomon insisted that I go all the way round.

'Give me a lift,' I said.

'Not today,' said Solomon said.

Then he drove away.

#

Donald and I are walking home because we missed the DEAN OF STUDENTS, MAKERERE UNIVERSITY, P.O. BOX 7062, KAMPALA. On Fridays, the DEAN OF STUDENTS shows up earlier than usual because, after that, it has to take matooke, charcoal, and other things (which our mothers need in plenty but which our fathers are too busy to buy) to the Freedom Square. If you are playing in the lower school compound by the time mzee parks the DEAN in the upper school compound, as Donald and I like to do on Fridays, mzee won't wait for you.

I picture my sister standing sentry in front of three bunches of matooke and a sack of charcoal, with her hands on her hips and her hot-combed hair wilting in the wind. I imagine her waiting for my mother to send my cousin to tell my brothers to stop playing football and carry the matooke home, and I also imagine her sulking because she would rather be playing tapo and kwepena with her friends.

Serves her right.

Donald asks for some of my glucose. He doesn't wait for my answer but wrests the sachet from my hand. I lick my fingers and watch him. Donald is my friend, but he can be mean. Sometimes, he spits on me. Sometimes, when he is with his friends, he calls me names. Sometimes, he slaps me on the back and pretends that he was trying to kill a mosquito. After that, he often tries to cheer me up with the *knock, knock, who is it, Amos, Amosquito* joke that stopped being funny last term.

Donald thrusts the sachet back into my hand after he discovers that there's no glucose left in it. He hits me with his bag and runs. After a while, he stops running and squats. When I finally catch up with him, I find him poking a stick into a pool of water. The harder the tadpoles try to escape, the more determined Donald is to stab them. Soon, though, he tires of the stabbing and tries to get a few ants that are marching past to fight each other.

Ever since he got that Sega Mega Drive, he's been trying to make the ant version of Streets of Rage. He has strange nicknames for his ant fighters. The small reddish-brown ones are 'Managers.' The ones with the long feelers and huge mandibles are 'Museveni's Men.' The ones with the smooth heads and long legs are 'Punishers.' The only ants that get to keep their real names in Donald's ant videogame are the sugar ants and black ants.

Donald is angry. Museveni's Man won't fight the Punisher. He tries to drown them both. No matter how much he tries, neither Museveni's Man nor the Punisher will drown. Donald throws the stick away and starts to look for a longer one. He doesn't seem to care that the sky is now the same colour as his skin was when he had measles. I care. I tug at his collar.

'What?'

'Let's go.'

'Wait.'

'Let's run to the embassy.'

'Isn't your other name Patience?'

My other name is Patricia and I do not want to wait. Not here. This part of our journey back home is always the quietest and loneliest. There are more gates here than people and the slim, silvery-green trees always look fed up and sad, as if they would rather be somewhere else.

'That's because this is a residential area,' Donald says.

Residential comes out of his mouth like a star-shaped Christmas decoration comes out of its box. As if I was not in class, seated right next to him, when Miss Nankabirwa used it in a sentence and wrote it on the blackboard. Residential area or not, this place, with its knotted knees and stomach-achey sounds, scares me. Sometimes I think I see faces peeping from behind the Mutuba tree.

'What if someone kidnaps us?'

'When will you stop being a coward?'

'Cowards live longer.'

'No one will kidnap us.'

'How do you know?'

'You have pierced ears and I have scars.'

'So?'

'Kidnappers want children without blemishes.

Witchdoctors can't sacrifice children with pierced ears and scars. It is against the rules. Don't you know anything?'

Blemishes.

Donald knows big words the way the tip of the tongue knows the gum. He knows how to pronounce them, too. In the reading test, he is the only one who knew how to pronounce island; he said 'eye land' and scored one hundred percent. I said 'eez land' and scored 98%. Bannange, how was I supposed to know the 's' was silent if no one had thought to tell me before?

I pull Donald's arm.

'What?'

'I have a secret.'

'What's it about?'

'You can't tell anyone.'

'How can I tell anyone if you haven't even told me anything yet?'

'Promise you won't tell anyone.'

Donald drops the stick and stands up. 'Is this about Mr. Lwanga having AIDS? If it is, I already know.'

'It's not. Promise me.'

'I promise.'

'You have to say it all or it won't mean anything.'

Donald mimes putting a padlock through his mouth. After he throws the key into the pool of water, he says, 'I promise I won't tell anyone.'

I take a deep breath and tell him that, even though Solomon is supposed to be dead, I sometimes see him in The Prevention. Donald's eyes grow wider than those of a mmese caught in a mousetrap. 'Say swear,' he says.

'Swear.'

Donald plays with his hair. 'Say the truth to ashame the devil.'

'I say the truth to ashame the devil.'

'Swear upon the living God.'

I can say swear but I am not supposed to swear upon anything. Instead, I wet a finger with saliva and mark the air the same way Mr. Lwanga marks the correct answers in my Kasuku exercise book.

'Swear upon the living God,' Donald insists.

I thrust my chest forward. 'Cross my heart.'

Donald looks square at me. 'If you are lying and I cross your heart, you will die.'

'I know.'

'After you die, you mustn't come to my house and bother me.'

'I won't come to your house.'

Donald shuffles his feet and scratches his head. 'Mpozi where is your heart?'

'Where it has always been.'

Donald makes the sign of the cross on my heart and waits to see if God will strike me dead. He doesn't.

'See. I wasn't lying.'

'Maybe God is busy,' Donald says.

'I swear upon the living God,' I say, finally,

knowing that this is the only way to convince Donald that I am not making things up. Donald stops walking and stares at me. He kicks his bag into the air. Then he spits into his hands and wipes them against his khaki shorts. 'Kale. When you see Solomon again, you tell me.'

'What will you do?'

'I will talk to him. Tell him you don't want to see him again.'

I hadn't said I didn't want to see Solomon again, but Donald sounds so sure that I don't want to see him, so I just say, 'Okay.'

Donald slings his bag onto his shoulder, looks at his Seiko watch, and grabs my arm. We run until we get to the embassy. We sit across from it, on the grass, and admire its green and white flag and gate.

'When I grow up, I am going to be an ambassador,' Donald says.

'When I grow up, I'm going to refuse to go to school. I'm tired of primary school.'

Donald assures me that primary school is only the beginning. 'We have to stay in school until university,' he says. Then he tells me that his parents told him that he'll go to university in outside countries. The Donalds are rich, very rich—last year, their other son's birthday party was at the Sheraton Kampala—but you would never know. You'll never hear him talking about all the cities he's been in. My mother likes that Donald does not show off. Actually, my mother likes Donald. If he didn't belong to a different tribe, she'd have liked him even more.

'Will you get married after university?' Donald asks.

I nod.

Donald wants to know who my husband will be.

'Prince William.'

Donald whacks me on the head. 'Don't be stupid,' he says. 'How will you get married to Prince William when you are already married to me?'

I hit Donald on the head with my bag. 'What makes you think I want to marry you?'

'I know you do,' he says.

'I want two children,' I say. 'Twins.'

'I want four children,' he says. 'Two boys and two girls.'

He pulls two lollipops out of his shirt pocket, carefully removes the shiny wrappers from both of them, and hands me one. While I suck on mine, I wonder whether I should ask Donald how many house-girls wash his shirts. He always leaves school with a brown shirt, as crispy as a dried leaf, and returns in the morning with one that is as white and soft as posho. Instead I ask him if it is true that kalodo, which I have seen some boys buy from the canteen on several occasions, is prepared in the cook's armpits.

Donald laughs. 'Wabula you're so stupid.'

'Naye ggwe,' I say, 'is stupid the only word you know?'

Donald doesn't answer my question, but says that he could make kalodo if he wanted, using the syrup produced by boiling juice from sugar cane. Now I really do feel stupid. So stupid that I do not tell him what else I've heard about kalodo. I overheard a girl tell her friend that kalodo is made from the saliva of the Indians that manage the sugar plantations.

Donald jumps up. 'The last one to the zebra crossing is a rotten kyenyanjja.'

From the way Donald flings himself down the hill, it is obvious that I am the rotten kyenyanjja. I stare at the gate to the embassy for a while, thinking about how much the green on the gate reminds me of the green of my sports uniform. And then, just as I stand up to follow Donald, I see The Prevention. As usual, Solomon is in the driver's seat. He parks The Prevention next to the embassy, then steps out and walks towards me. He asks how I am. I tell him I am fine. He says it is not safe for me to walk home alone. I tell him that I'm not really alone, that I was with Donald until I wasn't with him. Solomon picks up my bag and takes my hand. We walk together in silence for a while. Then Solomon lets go of my hand and hands me my bag. He says he is sorry.

'For what?' I ask.

For locking me in that room in the boys' quarters that afternoon, Solomon says. For almost doing something he should never have thought of doing in the first place, he adds. I can't remember anything about being locked in a boy's quarters, so I think about how much Donald might enjoy using 'in the first place' in a sentence. Solomon grabs my shoulders and says that if I do not forgive him, he will never rest. 'I forgive you,' I say, even though I am not sure what it is that I am forgiving.

'Thank you,' Solomon says. He walks back up the hill, enters The Prevention, and drives away. I walk until I find Donald waiting for me on the other side of the zebra crossing. He wants to know what took me so long. 'I was talking to Solomon,' I say.

'What? Didn't I tell you I'd talk to him?'

'Next time.'

There is no next time, though, because I never see Solomon again.

THE SAUSAGE TREE

Grace Neliya Gardner

My husband is Getemani and I, the woman he refers to so gently as "my wife", I'm Mazuwa. Getemani is a brown-skinned man of medium height, a muscular build and expressive eyes. He calls me his tall black beauty of grace. We live by the great Luangwa River on the edge of Mawuyu Village in Eastern Zambia, trying to fit neatly into the great system of flora and fauna with which we share the patch of earth.

We survive by the works of our hands. Getemani is a brave hunter and fisherman.He hunts buffalo, antelope, impala and occasionally, *njobvu* - the elephant. He also goes out fishing in the dugout canoe carved from the trunk of a baobab tree using the net I wove from reeds. Together, we cut up the game meat and fish, and then dry it before selling it.

Sadly this black beauty has a great grief. Though we have been married for ten years, I have not been able to give my husband a baby. I have watched the months pass, washing blood every turn of the moon. Many men would have taken a second wife by now but Getemani has resisted. Friends at the Shebeen tease him, saying, "Getemani, you are foolish. You have been bewitched by a barren woman." He laughs and tells them that one day I will give him a child and thereafter many more children.

It has not been easy for me. My soul teeters at the edge of an abyss whenever I hear such disparaging titters and whenever Tomaida, my close friend tells me she is pregnant.She has given birth three times after eight years of marriage and is now pregnant again.

Getemani and I were betrothed a few years after my initiation ceremony; I remember how young and innocent I was then. He was my hero, impressing the elders in my village near the Mozambique border, by bringing them large baskets of fish and dried game meat. He also paid the dowry without questioning the amount as other men usually did. That is why I am consumed with despair every time I think about my womb. "How can we fail to make a baby?"Sometimes I wonder if an evil spirit closed my womb and forced her to reject my husband's seed.

It was the season for grass cutting. Tomaida and I walked to the forest to cut some grass to thatch our huts. As we walked through the trees, Tomaida told me excitedly about her new baby whom she was expecting. The baby had started to move within her, so she could feel him.

"He?" I asked.

"Yes, I know he's a boy because I only wish to eat warthog and fish on the coals but not vegetables. I felt the same when I was pregnant with my late son."

For a moment, her face was clouded with sorrow. She lost one child to the dreaded malaria disease. He was only a year old.

"You are so lucky you have not experienced pains of childbirth then lose your child."

"You call me lucky? Not having a child is really bad. I envy you, Tomaida," I spoke softly.

Tomaida turned to me, her big eyes dripping with apology. I could see sympathy reflect in her pupils.

"I am sorry. I can't begin to imagine having no child. But my dear friend, have faith. You believe in the Great One up there,' she said pointing her index finger at the sky. He will bless you some day."

We continued to cut grass and we moved towards the lush patch near a clump of *chimvungulas* - sausage trees, each one of us wrapped in our own sad thoughts. We both cut five bundles of grass and stacked them under the nearby largest sausage tree. Afterwards, we sat in the shade to rest while drinking from our water bottles.

Suddenly from behind the bushes, we heard a faint sound as if light feet were treading on dry leaves. The sound increased and then I saw it.

"Hush, hush Tomaida - look, njobvu, elephant, there at the next tree!"

"Yes I see it Mazuwa. What shall we do? He'll crush us alive." Tomaida was terrified, so I held her close.

"He might not see us but he will smell us. Let's move before he comes closer."

We began to crawl as quietly as we could covering ourselves with some of the grass we had cut. When we were sure the distance between us and the elephant was safe, we ran across the flat open ground to the village path where we met three men. We were both breathing fast, especially pregnant Tomaida. She was clutching her belly

I called out, "Njobvu! We were seated under the chimvungula tree when it came and stopped at another large chimvungula tree close-by! We were lucky to get away."

"Elephants eat leaves and fruit of the chimvungula and tear the bark to taste the juice. You must be careful not to seat near sausage trees next time," the man replied. "Was it alone? A male?"

"It was a young male elephant," I answered.

"I wonder why it was alone. It must have left the restricted area; here it will be game for hunters." The men walked in the direction of the elephant as we walked to the village, more relaxed.

Later, when we were sitting together after our meal, I told my husband what had happened. He told me that the sausage tree was a favourite for many animals including giraffes, elephants and monkeys, Getemani commented. "You'd have been in more danger if the njobvu had been a female, especially one with young. The hunters say that female elephants can be more dangerous than the lion. I cannot imagine Tomaida running with her big belly!"

"Oh my husband, don't say that. She was exhausted and I was concerned for her," I rebuked him.

That evening, my husband set out on a fishing trip so I snuggled alone into the blankets on our reed sleeping mat. I had a vivid dream: I was walking towards the large sausage tree in the forest and it seemed to be beckoning to me. As I came nearer, the tree, it began to speak. It spoke in a deep intimate voice.

"I am the tree of wisdom, the tree of hope. Elephants, giraffes and monkeys multiply when they eat of my leaves, my fruit and my bark. Come, I will tell you something for your ears only."

I moved closer, fascinated.

"Take strips of my skin, my bark, soak them and drink the water. Do so for five days and believe in whatever you want to happen. I the chimvungula tree have spoken."

I woke up with a start and pondered as I lay in my warm nest. What was that; a dream about a talking sausage tree? It seemed so real. Creatures multiplying...

Getemani arrived home at daybreak and proudly told me that he had caught a large amount of fish, left to dry on the river bank in the charge of his young brother Jacko.

"My husband, I want to speak to you about something very important. Let us go and sit on our bed," I told him. We entered the hut and Getemani said "Mazuwa, Can this important secret wait? I want to have a bath."

"You will have a bath my husband. But first listen to me. I will fetch you the water, shortly. Now listen. I had a dream last night." I explained what had happened in my dream about the sausage tree. Getemani listened quietly. Then he said, "Matter of fact, medicine men and women also dream about the kind of trees to visit and pick their medicines from. Knowledge is imparted to human beings through dreams sometimes."

"Then maybe the tree is telling me something." I looked at him, wide-eyed. Getemani held my hand pressing my fingers tenderly, one by one. "Did you say the tree talked about animals multiplying because they eat its leaves, bark and fruit?" He laughed softly. I joined his laughter, nodding my head.

"Yes, that's what the tree told me. Maybe I should try and eat something from the tree and see what happens."

"Oh Mazuwa, no matter what people say or think, you are still my good wife. Sausage tree or no sausage tree," Getemani exclaimed.

This time it was my turn to squeeze his fingers one by one. He shifted his body towards me. I also moved closer to bridge the gap. That night my husband seemed like a different man, giving me time to discover and enjoy my womanhood. When we woke up later in the night, he asked, "Did I have a bath?"

"No. We forgot," I said snuggling closer.

The following day I asked my brother-in-law Jacko to escort me into the forest. I took a calabash, so I could collect water on the way back.

"Sister-in-law, they are saying that a njobvu has deserted the nearby game park and is in this vicinity." Jacko had fear in his voice.

"Yes, I know, we will be protected by our Father in the skies who watches over us."

We walked towards the clump of sausage trees. I went to the tree where we had left the bundles of grass and with my small knife, I chipped at the bark until I managed to get some strips; Jacko did not help me. He just stood watching me. I wrapped the strips in a small piece of cloth I had brought with me.

"Sister-in-law, what are those for?" he finally asked.

"It is for the pain I sometimes get in my stomach. Tomaida told me that a friend had used the same bark and was healed." We went on to the waterhole with the calabash to collect water.

"The water is very muddy today, Jacko",

I commented. He was standing a distance behind me, looking about nervously.

"Sister-in-law, hurry up! I heard a noise from the thicket where we came from." He looked scared. I collected the water and hoisted the calabash onto my head. We started off back home.

Suddenly, a bush pig crashed at full speed through the nearby bramble, rushing past us towards the clump of sausage trees. I lost my grip of my calabash and the water poured down over my head. All hell broke loose as a pack of wild dogs followed the course of the pig. The bush pig circled the sausage tree and tried to get away, but the wild dogs relentlessly pursued as the bush pig squealed in terror. We stood watching the drama for a few more minutes then started walking back towards the village. We were both afraid, not of the pig and dogs, but of the laws of the jungle and what else might be out there. I had only half a calabash of water left but luckily my cloth package was safe in Jacko's firm grip.

The following morning before sunrise, I took my package of sausage tree bark to the kitchen and put some of the bark strips into a cup of water to soak. For a moment, as I poured the water over the bark, I wondered why I was doing this strange thing, following dream of a sausage tree. But deep down I knew the answer; my desperation for a child would not let me leave any stone unturned if there was even a slight chance that it would yield fruit. I covered the concoction with a small plate and left it in the corner of the shelf out of the way. I decided to allow the bark to soak for some hours so that the spirit of the sausage tree would be active when I drank.

Next morning at dawn, I went into the kitchen and facing the direction of the big sausage tree, I took a few sips of the bark water. It was surprisingly sweet so I sipped some more, covered the cup and placed it back in the corner of the shelf.

I continued my bark-drinking ritual every morning. I found myself enjoying those peaceful moments in the cool early morning hours when I saluted the rising sun, turned to face the mother sausage tree and took my few sips. I realized I was sleeping better, my days were more peaceful and the nights with my husband filled with a new level of intimacy that left both of us satisfied. As we lay together on our reed mat and danced to the timeless tune of lovemaking, the night sounds became our lullaby.

On the fifth morning, I performed the last ritual and felt a heightened sense of excitement as I reflected on the fact that this was the time for my belief to be spoken. I walked down the path until I could see the branches of the sausage tree clearly. I then whispered into the fresh morning air, "I believe, I believe, great Creator Spirit. I am one with the trees, the animals and the birds. I beseech you for a baby!"

Then, feeling slightly foolish for talking to a tree I returned home, carrying secretly within me the knowledge that I had faithfully followed my dream as the tree had told me. I had heard her wisdom, carried my own hope and taken the leap of faith.

#

Five weeks later, I prepared a celebration meal, choosing large and succulent fish from my husband's baskets. I grilled the fish and served it with nshima and his favourite relish of dried mushrooms and wild onion from the river bank. Getemani was surprised by the meal. He said to me, "This is like a feast for a family gathering. What is the occasion?"

I smiled at my loving husband but wasn't ready to tell him my news yet.

(The Sausage Tree is adapted from a fable from Eastern Zambia)

QUEEN OF THE PEARLS

Linda Nkwoma Masi

It was near the end of November. The hazy sunshine and the dry, dusty and cold breeze announced the early return of the harmattan. My nostrils were like bath taps in a house long since disconnected from water supply as I sat in the cane chair by the window of our living room. The changes in the room stood out: freshly painted cream walls and new green damask curtains—long-service gift awards to Mama from the Covenant Mothers Home, an orphanage where she had served as a minder. The old settee with its worn upholstery was in place by the wall, the oak cot was in place beside the settee (Lucky Luke, my new ward, my precious pearl, lay asleep in it), and the lavender scent from the air freshener was so faint that the harmattan breeze smothered it. It was time for the 9 o'clock News Around the World, so I picked up the transistor radio from where it stood on the table and tuned in to Radio Nigeria 2 FM. There was a lot of hissing background noise but I still caught some of the news headlines: in England, the queen's diamond jubilee anniversary celebration was currently in preparation. And just then my mind tuned in to vivid memories etched in my heart—I remembered Sotonye, and suddenly my eyes were pools.

Sotonye was a jewel but I had always denied it.

One November night when I was about six years old, Mama returned home with a small bundle wrapped in a rice sack that stank like garbage. She had picked the bundle up from a garbage heap several blocks away from our house.

'Favour, turn on the hot tap, fast!' she said as she trudged to the bathroom.

'Yes, Mama!' I said, and then hobbled ahead of her as fast as my legs would allow. Mama walked with heavy steps not because of the bundle's weight but because she laboured to lift pounds of her flesh with each step she threw. She was a large woman.

I turned on the bath tap and rusty cold water spluttered out for a few moments. Then the water became clear and flowed smoothly. By the time Mama reached the bathroom, the water had turned warm. She opened the sack and brought out a bald, shrunken creature with many folds and lines in its purplish skin. It had a face like an old woman's and had tan ridges for eyebrows. It looked lifeless. She shook it vigorously but it remained motionless. Then she put its tiny feet under the flowing warm water, and after a moment, it kicked slowly and whimpered. 'She's alive!' Mama cried. 'Her name shall be Survivor Sotonye!'

Oh yes? *Born-throw 'way,* that's her second name, the nickname that the residents of Town (the area we lived, which was close by the Port Harcourt port) had for abandoned babies. I also was a Born-throw 'way. I was born with a cleft lip and a mangled right foot, and abandoned in an old carton at Mama's door. She made me her ward and named me Fighting Favour. And ever since, she became Mama to me.

Mama had a passion for charitable works; her home was a melting pot of abandoned babies. After finding me, she found other dumped babies. In her own words, we were like the biblical, proverbial pearls cast before swine—gifts to parents with blind minds—and so she called us pearls. But some of her pearls were eternally sick, and she later sent them off to the Covenant Mothers Home, leaving only me behind with her in her home, and that made me feel special. Our home was my palace: the place where I considered it my right to possess Mama's special attention. I didn't want anyone else to share that right with me, and I didn't want to be burdened with minding other, younger children. Then Sotonye was found.

For the first few days that Sotonye was in our home, Mama fed her with warm milk in a bottle, day and night, yet the little thing only looked purpler and shrank further. Then Mama took her to the Health Centre on the next street and there the mystery of her health was uncovered. Dr. Goodwill confirmed that her body lacked the normal ability to resist infection and that she had a deteriorating eye disease. He said she would go totally blind by the time she turned five years old. If she lived that long.

At four months old, Sotonye cried a lot more than any baby I had seen in our home, and Mama was always there to soothe her. Her cries gave me splitting headaches. Why wouldn't Mama just send her to the orphanage like the other children? She was stealing Mama's attention from me. She was an intruder!

One Sunday afternoon, Mama wanted to cook okra soup for lunch and asked me to keep an eye on Sotonye. The moment Mama dropped her in the cot in the living room and left for the kitchen, the little fiend began to cry—a nagging noise like a siren. I knelt by the cot and stuck my arm through the oak bars. Slowly, I swung my hand like a pendulum over her face to see if her round brown eyes followed my hand. For I had hatched a plan in my mind—to clamp her nose and mouth with my fingers long enough to stop the noise pollution that always sent Mama running to her side. This was the right moment to carry out my plan. But Sotonye stopped crying and reached out a tiny hand towards my hand. Her fragile fingers clutched my index finger, and then she babbled and grinned at me. Dimples appeared in her cheeks; her lips were pink and supple. I wished I had her dimpled smile. I tried smiling like her and felt the gap in my upper lip widen. I frowned and flung myself into the cane chair by the window. Thoughts of the imperfect face that stared back at me whenever I looked in a mirror filled my mind. I knew for certain that Mama was going to let her stay with us because of her smile.

Sotonye lived. She also remained in our home. She started calling Mama, Mama. She consumed tons of medicine everyday and grew like a coconut palm. When she turned five, she went totally blind, and my life took a crazy spin: I was stuck with her whenever I returned from school. She was like a sack of eggs tied to my neck, a fragile load of responsibility. I was determined to end her dependence on me but Mama continually drummed in my ears, 'Be a sister to her!' Those words seemed to realign my decision, though not for long. I soon discovered that man is like a coin. He has two faces, a good one and a bad one. He could pass one face off as another—with the exception of Mama, who had two good faces.

Sotonye now used a wheelchair because of her departed sight. I had to wheel her to any place of her bidding inside the house and at the backyard. I couldn't tell what Mama was afraid of—she forbade me from allowing Sotonye to be all by herself as though we were conjoined twins. The duty was a lot of bother, so I resolved to teach Sotonye to walk with a cane, without Mama's knowledge. Starting from the entrance door—fifteen steps straight on, a right turn and four steps—to the settee. From her bed—seven steps straight on, a left turn and two steps—to the bathroom door. She bumped into furniture countless times and almost gave up as many times, but I sang the promise of liberty of movement in her ears. Within a few months she had learned enough to move around without my help.

One evening, Mama returned from work looking exhausted. She sprawled on the settee in the living room and seemed to merge with it, only her halo of white spongy hair and rich cocoa skin making her distinguishable. (The tawny suede gown she wore matched the settee's upholstery.) I was sitting in the cane chair and staring at her dress when she asked me to get her a glass of water from the kitchen. Sotonye surprised us both by volunteering to get it, and after she jerked up from her wheelchair, she walked off with her eyes open and her cane tapping on the floor before her. After a few moments, she returned with a glass of water in her free hand. Mama was silent for some moments, and then tears fell down her cheeks as she bathed Sotonye with praises. When Sotonye spoke of the part I had played, Mama called me closer, then gripped my hands and shook them such that my whole body quaked while she poured blessings on me. Finally she said, 'Good work, Favour!' I nodded my thanks, unable to speak. I felt like a sooty kettle coated with talcum powder. If Mama could open my heart she would see that my good work was only for myself—to cast off my 'burden.'

One January afternoon, despite the thorough hygiene rules we observed at home, a housefly buzzed to our dining table as we were having lunch. I beat the air to keep it from settling on the mound of eba and melon soup in my bowl. It eventually landed on the food in Sotonye's bowl. That same moment Mama appeared from the kitchen and saw it. She screamed as though there was a man pointing a loaded revolver at Sotonye's temple. *A common housefly?* I thought, and watched as Mama grabbed a broom and succeeded in striking the fly against the wall to its untimely demise. 'Diarrhoea distributor!' Mama said and walked off to the kitchen with Sotonye's bowl. I heard a thud as the eba landed inside the waste bin. A moment later, she returned with another bowl of eba for Sotonye, and then, with a stern look at me, she said, 'Favour, I'm sure you could have done something about that fly!'

I swallowed the eba in my mouth and said, 'I—I'm sorry, Mama! I'll be more observant next time.'

By the time Sotonye was about nine years old (we counted our years by our various found-dates), she had mastered the use of her cane both inside the house and around the backyard. But she sprained her left ankle during the last week of her training and was confined to her wheelchair, taking forever to heal. A minor ankle sprain! What a waste of effort! Her confinement to a wheelchair did not even dampen her spirits. She had developed in many ways. She was already far into her first term in Braille school and had also grown quite confident in the knowledge she acquired there. During her spare time, she read *Vision*, a fat book, with the tips of her fingers, and whenever Dr. Goodwill paid us a home visit, she engaged him in conversation and asked him loads of questions about everything. Their twittering always left him misty-eyed.

Sotonye was tall for her age, almost the same height as I was, but she was skinny, this maybe because she so ate little. She had no idea how pretty she looked, and certainly I wasn't going to be her talking mirror. I wished I had her straight legs, though. She had also developed the habit of listening to Radio Nigeria 2 FM on the transistor radio in the living room. Apart from listening to the music, her favourite program was the 9 o'clock News Around the World. News was like schoolwork. What a bore! Earlier in the week, she had gathered from the news that the queen of England would celebrate her golden jubilee anniversary the following year. Later that same day, a program called Britain's Reigning Monarch at Seventy-Five was shown on TV. From the moment Sotonye heard of the program, she began harassing me with questions that tumbled out of her mouth. *Tell me, Favour, is the queen tall or short? She doesn't look stern, does she? What's the colour of her coat?* I had become her eyes and that was a burden to me. I wished she would just melt away like Nwamanu in a folktale Mama once told. Nwamanu was the most beautiful girl in Alioma Kingdom and she was made out of red palm oil. Her father spared her from every hard work, especially work that involved fire. But the day before her marriage to the prince of the land, when her father went hunting, her wicked stepmother forced her to make a fire for their dinner. Nwamanu obeyed and set the firewood; the moment she lit the fire, she melted into palm oil and vanished.

#

Three days later, Sotonye was still talking about the queen: how she got married at the age of twenty-one, how she was involved with about six hundred charities around the world, the list went on. I was tempted to call Sotonye the queen of British news, but I thought of something even more interesting.

The next day, November 10, was Sotonye's found-day anniversary. After her bath, I helped her dress up in the most hideous attire I could find in a basket of disused clothes—my old, ink-stained, pink linen gown and one of Mama's discarded Afro wigs that was a mass of tangles. Afterwards, her voice brimming with excitement, she asked me, 'So how do I look?'

'You look like the queen of the pearls!' I piped.

Her joy touched the bedroom ceiling as she thanked me for dressing her up. I went to the living room to laugh my head off. I didn't know that she had wheeled her chair after me until I heard her bump into the occasional table. I turned and my laughter died. In her right palm lay the diamanté bangle she had won at the Port Harcourt Trade Fair lottery last December.

'Favour!'

'Uh-huh.'

'I want to properly thank you for being a dear sister to me,' she said in a silken voice. 'I would like you to have this bangle. Mama says it's very beautiful but I can't see it. I think it would be of better value to you.'

I didn't know when I burst into tears. What a shame I was.

To mark Sotonye's found-day anniversary, Mama cooked palm oil rice and smoked sardine for dinner and told us folktales after our meal. Later that night, there was a power cut. The loud whirring of some neighbour's generator filled the small room I shared with Sotonye. The moonlight reached into the room through the curtains and tinted everything it touched. I could see the fan hanging from the ceiling like a pale wreath. Sotonye and I slept in separate beds under white mosquito nets to keep the bloodsuckers away, but the nets were also like cages. I felt hot. I flung off my sweat-soaked nightdress and remained wearing only my underwear. Then I improvised a fan out of one of my school notebooks, but it only produced a current of hot air. I sighed from the heat.

'Favour, are you still awake?' Sotonye said in the darkness. After I answered with a grunt, she chuckled and said, 'I was just wondering what my life would be like when I'm twenty-one.'

You're just nine for heaven's sake, I wanted to shout. I knew that this was a spillover from the news about the queen of England.

'I think Mama is like the queen,' Sotonye said. 'How she does all this kind, charitable work helping abandoned babies. I want to be like her! So what goal do you hope to achieve by the time you're twenty-one?'

Up until that moment, I had not given any serious thought to what kind of future I wanted for myself. I stared at the side of my mosquito net as though it was a whiteboard which had the answers I sought written on it. And with seeming mockery of my expectation, its tiny holes shaded by the room's moonlit darkness stood out like words. Words that described the holes in the net, but, shockingly, also described the emotions I battled with in the deep recesses of my heart: dark—empty. I didn't know what to say to Sotonye. I felt embarrassed, and then angry at her because her question had made me feel embarrassed.

'I feel sleepy. Go to sleep!' I said.

#

One week later, I sat on the settee in the living room, knitting a woollen purse for myself. My knitting needles clacked rhythmically.

'Favour, please knit one for me too,' Sotonye said. She was seated in her wheelchair beside me.

'Here, learn!' I said, shoving spare needles and a ball of red wool into her hands in her lap. *You want everything!*

She pushed out her lips in an angry pout and her eyes blinked rapidly for a moment. Then she exhaled deeply and her thin shoulders relaxed. 'Okay, please, teach me,' she said.

By the next week, when Sotonye had learned to knit silly playthings for herself, we were studying in our room when she paused in her reading and suggested that we should knit accessories, ones that were fit for the harmattan, for Mama. Her idea sailed above my imagination. How come I had never thought of knitting a gift for Mama?

'So what do you think of the suggestion?' Sotonye said.

'Mama will be glad,' I said quietly.

A confident smile lit Sotonye's face.
If she was fishing for compliments from me, she had cast her net in the wrong ocean. I felt such an idiot, and this feeling caused antagonism to boil up inside me. Sotonye decided to knit a scarf for Mama, and I made sure I

knotted red, purple and teal wool for her, all colours I disliked. I hoped the scarf would turn out ugly. I knitted a cream bobble hat and decorated it with wooden beads.

Four days later, Mama was on her way out for her evening shift at work when I caught up with her in the living room and gave her the hat. She loved it instantly. Her soft arms wiggled as she threw them about my shoulders, then she planted a warm kiss on my forehead. The smell of her fuchsia deodorant lingered on the sleeves of my blouse. Mama was delighted when Sotonye offered her the scarf. She leaned forward, hugged Sotonye, and gave her a smacker on the forehead. When she straightened up there were trails of tears along her cheeks.

'My pearls, thank you so much!' she said with a ring in her voice.

She donned both accessories and didn't mind the outrageous scarf at all. Then she asked me to fetch the kerosene container for her. My eyes clouded as I headed to the kitchen. I wondered why she did not shed tears when she had received my own gift. While I emptied the remaining kerosene out of the blue, plastic jerrycan into the lamp, I heard her complaining that the cost of kerosene had rocketed. After I returned and handed her the jerrycan, she left.

Later that evening at our backyard, Sotonye sat in her wheelchair while I sat on a plastic stool, stuck with her as usual. We were eating mangoes. The sun looked like a giant orange trapped in an azure sea. It left a reddish glow on the zinc roof of our neighbour's bungalow that stood beyond the fence. Our backyard was a short stretch of concrete floor with a clothesline and posts.

Sotonye spoke. 'Favour, do you think Mama really loved the scarf I made for her?'

'Why do you ask?' I said and bit into the juicy flesh of my mango.

'Her tears dropped on my arms when she hugged me,' Sotonye said.

I stared at her in disbelief. *Of course she was enraptured by your gift,* I wanted to shout. Instead, in a strained voice, I said, 'Maybe she was thinking of the things bothering her.'

'Oh no . . . Mama's bothered?' Sotonye cried.

In trying to keep the truth from Sotonye, I told her things that made her begin to worry at Mama's workload. She then conceived the idea of volunteering to work at the orphanage during the Christmas holidays with Mama. A little volunteer! I felt jealous. And worse, she would be spending more time with Mama at work. Why hadn't I thought of volunteering in the first place? Not that I cared about that kind of donkey work, anyway.

I fixed Sotonye a glare and just then noticed a large, greenish housefly perched on the yellow flesh of her mango. I flicked my hand at the fly and it buzzed lazily away. 'A fly?' Sotonye cried in alarm. 'Did it perch on my mango?'

'No!' I lied, and guiltily turned my face away from her even though I knew I was safe from her wide sightless eyes. *If she doubts me,* I thought, *she should go and dispose of her mango in the bin and get another one for herself.* I wasn't Mama! She had succeeded in stealing Mama's attention at home and now she wanted to extend her thievery to the orphanage.

We both continued eating our mangoes.

About 7 o'clock that evening, Mama called to say that she would be home late because of an emergency with one of the children at the orphanage. Sotonye and I retired early because there was a power cut. The kerosene lamp was in a corner of our room. Its small yellow flame gave off a dull light that made my eyes heavy with sleep. I had shut my eyes for only a few minutes when Sotonye suddenly cried, 'Favour! Favour!'

'Eh?' I sat up with a jolt.

'I feel sick! I want to throw up!' she cried. She was seated at the edge of her bed and her feet were on the floor.

'Just hold on! I'll get a bucket!'

I ran to the bathroom and got a bucket. As I held it up for her, she vomited. The next moment she said she wanted to go to the toilet. I led her there. While waste matter flowed from her bowels, she said she wanted to throw up. Again? I got the bucket. She was pumping vomit out of her mouth and waste matter out of her bowels at the same time. Her retching racked her lean body. I could smell an essence of mango in her vomit.

'It's diarrhoea, isn't it?' she cried.

Guilt coursed through me as I thought of the housefly that had perched on her mango. 'Anything could have caused it, I've had it before, you'll soon beat it,' I said, holding my breath at intervals as I suppressed the sick feeling in my stomach. The smell of her vomit and faeces was too much for me to bear. Yet I didn't think there was any cause for alarm. In an hour or two she should be all right.

Her bowels flowed.

She vomited.

'I feel dizzy and weak,' she cried. 'My stomach hurts!'

'I'm sorry! I'll go and prepare a sugar and salt solution for you—but first I'll call Mama.'

'Okay . . . Favour! Please come back soon.'

'I will.'

While she was still squatted over the toilet bowl, I went to get my cell phone from my bedside drawer. I called and told Mama about Sotonye's ailment. For the few minutes she spoke, she released a fusillade of jumbled up exclamations, questions, commands and declarations at me—the long and short of it being that she was returning home immediately and bringing Dr. Goodwill with her.

Mama had taught me the correct measurements of a sugar and salt solution that could pass for an oral rehydration therapy in emergencies. When I gave Sotonye the solution in a glass and she vomited it up, my heart jumped. It was supposed to work like magic. I stared at her as though she was an alien from Mars.

'I feel cold . . . I can't feel my hands and my feet,' Sotonye cried.

'Lean against the cistern and try not to think of how you feel. Think of something pleasant,' I said. I dialled Mama's number again and again but there was no connectivity. Sotonye kept vomiting and retching. Then she started crying.

'I'm sorry!' I said, patting her shoulder gently. The more I felt sorry for her, the more I wanted to be someplace else. Far away from her. And then the lamplight started blinking like the eyes of an old man who was fighting off sleep. Argh! Mama was supposed to return with more kerosene!

There was knocking at the front door.

'Sotonye, someone is at the door,' I said.

'Okay! Please come back soon,' she said.

'I will!' I replied, and left for the living room, taking the lamp along with me.

The man at the door had missed his way. He was looking for our next-door neighbour, so I directed him to the right door. Then I sank into the cane chair in the living room and began gulping in the lavender-scented air.

Sotonye called my name twice but I didn't answer. The smell of the vomit and faeces in the toilet was disgusting, but, really, it was the guilt for her suffering that bound me to the chair. Why hadn't I helped her to throw away that silly mango? Tears clouded my eyes. Moments later, the lamplight started blinking continuously. I shook the lamp and found that it was empty. I returned to the toilet to find Sotonye sitting with her back rested against the cistern. Was she practicing to sit like the queen even in the toilet?

'Sotonye!' I shouted. She didn't answer. I reached out and shook her shoulder. It felt cold to the touch, and suddenly she crashed sideways to the floor. Her head fell backwards in an awkward manner. She looked pale in the lamplight; her legs and arms were like sticks.

'Sotonye?'

She lay so still. Fear gripped my heart. I knelt by her side and felt her heart for a beat, but there was none. I felt her wrist for a pulse and there was none, too.

'Oh God! Sotonye!'

I gathered her little body that had always been weightless like paper in my arms. I reached out and wagged her silken plait, hoping for a smile, her perfect smile. Her lips were thin ashen blocks. I felt my chest knot with pain and for a moment I could not breathe. A croaky sound escaped my throat and tears streamed down my face. The lamplight blinked twice and went out, plunging me into darkness. The last dim yellow flicker of the light reminded me now and forever of Sotonye's yellow mango.

RECONSTRUCTION

Doreen Anyango

They never tell you the whole story. They tell you that you may experience nausea and or diarrhoea. They don't tell you that you will feel like your innards are forcing their way out of your body in two different directions at the exact same time. They tell you that you may experience skin irritation from the radiation. They don't tell you about the ugly blisters and how what used to be your breast will feel like it's on fire. They tell you that you may experience weight loss and hair loss, these in addition to the breast you've already lost to the scalpel. They don't tell you that you will feel like your body is disintegrating right before your very eyes. Or that you will look in the mirror and death will stare back at you.

This is exactly how I feel as I stare at my emaciated, toxin-filled, maimed self. And at the clump of hair in my hands, another bit of my crowning glory that is now falling out with reckless abandon. And then I start to scream. And then my mother is bursting through the door in her night gown. And she is holding me tightly to herself, and we are sitting on the bathroom floor still entwined. And she is trying to pry my fingers open and remove the hair. And I am tightening my grip and shouting, *it's mine, it's mine.* And then she is cooing in my ear like I am a little baby and gently rubbing my back. And then I am not screaming any more. I am lying on my bed and staring at the wall and she is seated on the chair by my bedside and looking at me. I can't see her face, but I feel her eyes on my back like two laser beams. I feel exhausted.

Growing up, my mother always said that I didn't know what my brain was for. The few times she helped me with my homework were akin to torture sessions. *Think, think, think*, she'd say, wagging a finger at me. I'd just look at her with what she called my blank look and she'd always give up in frustration. She'd be glad to know that I finally figured out how to think. That thinking is all I do these days.

I have thought about my gravestone in Rutooma, right next to my dad's. I want a heart-shaped one with a fat baby angel engraved on it—for my miscarried baby that did not get a funeral. I have thought of the perfect epitaph:

Greta Nadine Rukundo

08.07.1987 – pretty soon from the look of things

She could have thought more

I have thought about how, if it's true what they say, that it's in adversity that we know who our true friends are. My mother, who I have been at loggerheads with from as far back as I can remember, is my true friend, and a husband I fought for and defended and married against the wishes of practically everybody I know, is not. She's taken me in and given me a comfortable place to stay. She has made sure I get treatment: using her doctor connections to make sure I am treated by one of the top oncologists in the country and then driving me to every single radiation and chemotherapy session, and also bullying and bribing the nurses to make sure I never have to queue. She's made sure I get nourishment: feeding me all manner of herbs and vegetables in a concoction so pungent I have to drink it from a closed bottle with a straw so I don't have to smell it. My husband on the other hand seems to have fallen off the face of the earth. I have not heard from him for six months now. Thinking of him fills me with a rage of such intensity that my head starts to feel like it will explode. I have tried without any success to not hate him, to try and see myself from his point of view. Hell, I would leave me too if I could. But I can't. And so I am stuck in this dark and lonely and infinitely terrifying place. And he should be here with me. Isn't that what husbands are supposed to do . . . in sickness and in health and all that bullshit?

Incidentally, I would never have met Ally if it wasn't for my mother. She'd entered the living room one afternoon as I watched a local dance competition on the TV, then snorted and made a comment to the effect that the kids taking part in the competition were wild. I had just turned eighteen at the time, and was enduring my long S6 vacation while also bored to within an inch of my life. It was too late to join the competition, but I decided I was going to be a dancer. And so I joined a dance group.

I remember the first time I saw his tall lean frame leaning on the dance studio mirror. He was chatting with a short girl who had her head tilted back at an uncomfortable angle that only he, could look at her face. He saw me hovering by the door and smiled at me over the girl's head. Then walked over, still smiling. 'Hi, I'm Ally,' he'd said and held out his hand to me. His palm was soft but the handshake was firm. I took in the curly Afro. The thick, arched eyebrows and the long eyelashes. The eyes that were just the right amount of big—any bigger and they'd be too big. The lopsided grin and the dimple in his left cheek.

At twenty-three, Ally was the oldest of the group of four guys and two girls from the slum area of Kisenyi, all of them with big dreams of stardom. Although not the best dancer, he was by far the most ambitious. He was also the most educated, having actually completed high school. As a perceived rich kid, I was met with hostility from some members of the group. I was merely tolerated in spite of my talent and allowed to remain in the group only because Ally always stood up for me. For my part, I was enchanted by him. And so when it was time to leave for university, I chose not to go. My mother was livid. She threw me out of the house and I went to live in the shared house of the dance group, a rundown two-bedroom apartment in Kireka. I had the choice of either sharing a bed with one of the girls or sleeping on the floor. I chose the floor. That first night, unable to sleep on the barely-there mattress that was spread on the floor, I kept hoping my mother would storm the place with policemen and force me back home. She didn't.

Ally took me under his wing and introduced me to sex and hard liquor and marijuana. I got pregnant at twenty, when I should have been in my second year at the university. I wasn't sure I was ready to be a mother, but Ally was all for it, so I let him be sure for both of us. But I miscarried when the pregnancy was four months old. A few weeks after the miscarriage, we got married at the registrar's office. We left the group house and went to live in our own place. Ally concentrated on talent management, just the dance group initially, but with time his portfolio grew to include several well-regarded local artistes. I took on some modelling jobs: catwalk, print, billboards, TV ads, and the bane of my mother's existence, music videos.

When we were recently married, Ally had tried hard to bridge the gap between my mother and me, and hoped that in the process he would somehow earn her approval. I told him that trying to win my mother's approval was like attempting to catch the wind, but he was determined to make her acknowledge him. He would insist on us visiting her at home every once in a while, 'like normal people.' On the few occasions I agreed to these visits, she never spoke to him directly. She'd respond to his greetings with a nod and then ignore him completely. She would speak only in Runyankore so he didn't understand a thing. She never said his name and had her own way of referring to him. *That terrorist you call a husband,* she would say to me. *That refugee you married. That ka Somali of yours.* Ally eventually got tired of being humiliated and stopped pestering me to 'go see mummy.'

Ally hit the jackpot when he went into event promotion and management. We left our modest two-roomed house and moved into a fancy apartment in a posh neighbourhood. But success seemed to diminish him somehow. The spark that had drawn me to him in the earlier days was replaced by a bigger waistline and the arrogant air of someone who had 'made it.' In the days before I found the lump, I'd often caught myself struggling to remember why I ever thought there was anything special about him.

I checked into the hospital for the mastectomy with Ally by my side. He was being a caring, attentive husband, and there was such dejection in his eyes that one would have thought it was his breast that was going to be cut off. I woke up on the other side of the operation to an annoyingly cheerful nurse who informed me that the surgery had gone well. I am sure I would have spat in her face if I hadn't seen my mother lurking in the doorway. I had given express instructions to Ally not to call her. I looked around for Ally, but before I could ask the question, my mother said, 'He's gone.' I was about to ask the next question when she added matter-of-fact: 'He called me. Said he had to dash to Cape Town for some urgent business.' Her arms were folded across her chest, her voice level, her face devoid of emotion. I just stared at her while a huge block of ice took residence in my stomach. I could feel a dull ache under the thick layer of bandages on my chest as I closed my eyes. I wished I was somewhere else, anywhere else.

Being back in the house I grew up in has made memories of my dad and my brother Donald return. Most of my happy childhood memories involve the two of them. Everybody thought my dad was mad. I thought he was merely happy. Although I was sometimes confused by his particular brand of happiness that involved walking down the street in his underwear and shouting at the top of his voice about utopia, I defended him with all the conviction of a nine-year-old, even getting into physical fights with neighbourhood kids who laughed at him. At other times he stayed in his bedroom, scribbling furiously in a notebook or muttering quietly to himself. I went to his bedroom every day after school. I'd tell him about my day and he'd tell me stories. What I understood from his stories was that there was a wonderful place called utopia where only happy people lived and good monsters with magical powers ruled and that he and I would go there one day. He'd go on and on for hours and I'd listen enraptured. There were also some days when he didn't feel like talking and we'd just sit in silence and listen to Bob Marley until the maid came to get me.

My dad lived in the boys' quarters with his mother Kaka, his sister Aunt Kemi, and her two kids. In the main house my mother lived with my brother and I, as well as a maid and an assortment of visiting relatives from her side of the family. The two houses were like neighbouring countries at war. The buildings were separated by a narrow walkway not more than a meter wide, thus it was hard to stay out of each other's way, and so battles happened regularly. It didn't take much for full-blown chaos to break out. It was either that one of Aunt Kemi's kids sat on our veranda, or our maid looked at Aunt Kemi in a way she did not appreciate, or one of their chickens strayed into our kitchen. Once, my maternal grandmother and paternal grandmother almost came to blows over a mixing stick. Only I was allowed to move freely between the two houses. As a punishment for some offence I can't remember, my mother once forbade me to go on my daily visit, and because of this my dad waylaid her as she left for work the following morning and threatened to cut her to pieces with a machete.

My dad's side liked to have parties in the shared compound. All kinds of occasions were celebrated, from graduations to birthdays to baptisms and confirmations, and many times there were even just-for-the-hell-of-it parties. They'd have them on any day of the week without warning. We'd come back from school to a tent in the compound and blaring music. These parties were major feasts every time with lots of sodas, lots of booze, and lots of roast meat and they went on till the early hours of the morning. When my mother was around, she would curse and jeer and turn off the security lights so that they were in darkness. They would connect lights from their house and turn up the volume of the conversation and the laughter and the music. On such occasion, I'd lock my bedroom door and attend the party through the window. My cousins would then bring me soda and meat and balloons. When mother would not be around, my brother Don would let me stay at the parties until midnight.

My mother was away so much that Don pretty much became the mother. He woke me up in the morning to prepare for school. He made sure I had breakfast and took me to school at Kitante Primary School before proceeding to Makerere College School where he studied. He'd pick me up in the evening and would ask about my day and listen to me talk all the way back home. When we would get home, he'd go to his room while I went to see dad. He'd then send the maid to get me when it was time for supper, after which he'd help me with my homework and make sure I had a bath and brushed my teeth before going to bed. If anybody needed anything around the house, they consulted him. Back then, the role of head of the house seemed perfect for him. It's only now as an adult that I realize how much responsibility it must have been for a shy and quiet teenager to take on.

Don seemed to live beyond all the chaos and drama in our household, and most of the time he had his face buried in a book and with headphones firmly plugged into his ears. All our conversations were question and answer sessions, with him asking brief questions and listening to my long-winded answers, or me bombarding him with a barrage of questions that he answered either with a nod, a shake of the head, a shrug, a smile or, if I was very lucky, a laugh. I thought him sad and my biggest wish was for him to be happy like me and dad. I often made up funny stories and also embellished some of my dad's just to make him laugh. His laugh sounded like someone choking under water, as his whole body would shake from the muted force of it and there'd be tears in his eyes. Even his happy seemed a little sad.

But he'd talk to my mother, and he didn't sound sad then. Every day when she was around, after supper he'd send me off to bed and they'd have tea and talk, just the two of them. Sometimes I would sneak back and listen to them while lying on the floor in the corridor. He'd first go over matters of the house. *We are running out of rice. Greta has to go on a school trip to the airport next week and she wants sports shoes and a purple dress. The electricity bill came. The grass needs to be cut.* Then he'd tell her about school, how one kid nearly got her face burnt in a chemistry experiment gone wrong. She'd in turn tell him about work, and about how she'd nearly run over a cat in the parking lot and about the nurse from the north with the weird accent and attitude. *What did she do this time?* he'd ask, and they'd laugh together over her response. All this time I'd be feeling left out and jealous.

Two weeks after my tenth birthday, my dad hanged himself in his bedroom. The bus dropped me off after school (Don had entered university by this time and I now used a school bus service) and when I saw cars parked outside our compound, I assumed it was a party. But there was no music. My dad's side of the family was gathered in the same party tent as always. Aunt Kemi and Kaka and several of the other women were sobbing, while my dad, always the life of the party, was nowhere to be seen. When they saw me, they all broke into loud wails.

A few months after my dad's funeral, Donald, who was then a first-year student of medicine, overdosed on a concoction of drugs. His roommate tried but failed to wake him up one morning. He had left a note by his bed that simply said: I can't do this anymore. Don's funeral was a quiet affair in a cemetery with a few of mother's relatives and his friends from school. I remember feeling an overwhelming sense of doom as I watched his casket being lowered into the ground. When we got home, I locked myself in my bedroom and cried so long and hard that I thought my stock of tears would run out. But I never saw my mother shed a tear over his passing, not even once.

After Don's funeral, my mother stayed around for much longer than usual. She seemed to have no idea what to do with me. This made me even more awkward around her. I was afraid to talk for fear of saying the wrong thing. I spoke only when spoken to and then only in monosyllables. My mother was frustrated by this and her refrain of *think, think, think* was replaced by *speak, speak, speak up!* This she would say in a high-pitched voice that rendered me incapable of coherent speech. When the school year ended, the perfect solution was found. I was sent away to boarding school and my mother and I continued being strangers to each other.

During the months I have been living here since my mastectomy, I have had to contend with much longer periods of silence than I am used to. My mother, a maid and I are the only ones in the house. My mother and I have never had much to say to each other, and the maid says so little that for the first few weeks I was here I even thought she was mute. Also, she has the biggest eyes I have ever seen in my entire life. Whenever I look at her I imagine they will pop out at any moment and start rolling about on the floor. I don't want to be present when that happens, so I keep my distance. I sort of enjoyed the silence in the early days, but these days when it drags on for too long, strange things start to happen. I sometimes hear my dad's voice, or I feel Don's presence so strongly that I begin to imagine he is sitting right next to me. Right now I feel empty, as if I have only air on the inside. I feel like I am weightless and floating among the clouds, not lying on this bed curled up and staring at a blank wall.

'I never know what to say to you,' my mother says, startling me.

'No shit, Mother,' I say and roll over on the bed so I can see her flinch. My mother has a physical reaction to bad language, and even now, she doesn't disappoint.

She seems to be thinking about what to say for a while, and then, 'I was happy once, you know.'

'*Right,*' I say.

She stands up from the chair and leaves quickly. As I start to drift off to sleep, she walks back into the room with a big stack of books. She sits on the bed and signals for me to sit up and come closer. After obeying, I notice that almost her entire hair has turned grey.

'Eh, Mother, you're old,' I say.

'Hm. What is it you used to say to me? While you were away I grew up, that's it,' she says and hands me one of the big books. It is a photo album. On the first page is a black and white picture of my mother and my dad. She is wearing a short dress and heavy shoes. She has a huge Afro with a single flower stuck behind one ear. My dad is so much taller than her; he towers over her and has an arm draped around her shoulder as if in protection. He has on bell bottom trousers, a flower-patterned shirt, and a dark hat placed at an angle on his Afro. My mother is smiling into the camera and my dad is smiling his cheeky grin into her hair. 'That's us in medical school,' my mother says. I can't think of anything to say and so I continue flipping through the album, all the while listening to her running commentary. At graduation. At a party somewhere sometime, both sitting close together and surrounded by bottles and happy faces. A few wedding photos: my mother in a loose-fitting white lace dress with a puffy sleeves and a huge bow at the waist, my dad in a black suit and a bow tie. Dressed in winter clothes with snow in the background—*doing our masters in the UK*. Wearing identical hideous sweaters while seated side by side in each other's arms under a brightly decorated Christmas tree in—*I am pregnant with Donald there*. Dad in a doctor's coat with a stethoscope around his neck. And lots of pictures of Don. Don as a newborn, Don sitting, Don crawling, Don smiling into the camera with two teeth. Don standing up and supporting himself on a stool. Don in a kindergarten playground with lots of white kids. Don hoisted up on my dad's shoulders.

I am nowhere in the pictures. Clearly I was a post-happiness event.

'So what happened?' I ask, closing the last of the photo albums. 'How did we end up living in a warzone?'

'We were too different in the end, I think, your

dad and I. I am too uptight, as you like to say. Your dad was too . . .'

'Downloose?' I say.

She chuckles. 'I think perhaps one should stick to one's own kind.'

'Two downloose people is a circus, Mother. Trust me.'

She remains quiet for some time. 'Anyway, your dad's mental state started to deteriorate while we were still in the UK. We got him psychiatric help and with the right medication, his condition was under control. But he couldn't continue work as a doctor and so he insisted on coming back home. I was pregnant with you at the time, so I figured that maybe it was time to come and settle back home. We had always said we'd come back to settle after the war ended. I was doing my first PhD at the time . . .'

I interrupted her. 'Wait, your first? You have more than one PhD?'

'Yes. I have two,' she says with not a little pride.

'You're allowed to do that?'

'You can get as many as you want.'

'Right . . .'

She gives me a familiar look—the one that expresses incredulity at our being related. 'So, anyway,' she continues, 'I took a break to move back home. Then we bought this house and your dad got a job lecturing at the medical school while I set up a home for us.' Her voice trails off. She seems lost in her thoughts, a wistful smile on her lips. I say nothing until she resumes speaking. 'And then you were born and everything was good. I decided to go back and finish my studies when you were about a year old. Your dad didn't want me to go, but I did anyway. Things changed after that. I came home to find that your dad's relatives had somehow managed to convince him that the cause of his mental illness was witchcraft and that I was the one behind it.'

'Witchcraft! Seriously?'

'You mean you didn't know? I always assumed somebody told you.'

'No, I didn't know,' I say, and then remember how he always got so angry whenever I mentioned the word *mother*. 'But that explains why dad hated you so much.'

'I hated this place,' she says. 'And yet I couldn't leave. I still can't leave.' She shakes her head sadly.

'But you did leave. I remember you leaving a lot. Where did you always go? Don was almost my mum.'

'It was work. I was working on several international research projects and I'd attend all these conferences connected with that. I was also studying for my second PhD.' She is silent a while and then exhales slowly. 'But I always came back.'

'Yes,' I say.

'Don was the biggest victim of it all,' she says and starts wringing her hands and rocking back and forth.

'I should have left for Don. I should never have made him choose.'

Left for Don or left with Don, I wonder silently. What about me?

'He was so close to his dad in the early years. He knew happier days and I think that made it harder for him when things fell apart. You on the other hand grew up with the chaos.'

'Well, I survived.'

'You did.' she says, looking up at the ceiling, and then she reaches out her hand and pats me on the knee. I am suddenly aware of how close together we are sitting. She smells of talcum powder.

'You know, you remind me of your dad in the earlier days,' she says, her gaze still fixed on the ceiling. 'And you smile just like him too.'

That wistful little smile again. I feel like a stranger who is looking in on an intensely private moment. I decide to remain silent and not intrude. And then a thought occurs to me.

'Do you think I will also run mad like him? God has given me cancer . . . surely he will spare me madness.'

She laughs and says, 'You know, before this whole cancer business and getting to know you, I thought you had already started running mad.'

'That's not nice!' I say with a laugh and pinch her on the arm.

'I'm sure you will be fine,' she says, rubbing her arm, and finally drops her gaze from the ceiling. An awkward silence hangs between us. I have heard my mother laugh and joke around before, so I know it is within the realm of possibility. It has just never happened with me before.

'I regret so much,' she says in a serious tone. 'I lost my husband and my only son. And now my only daughter hates me.' She turns to face me and looks me directly in the eyes. Her face is only inches from mine. Looking at her, I don't see anger or bitterness, just a deep sadness. There's an almost beseeching look in her eyes. I want to say to her, *I don't hate you, really I don't.* But the words won't come. Instead I am thinking that this is weird, that she needs to leave me alone, at least for now. I don't say it, but maybe I think it so loud that she hears it. And so she stands up from bed, gathers up her happy memories, and leaves.

MY FAULT

Monica Cheru-Mpambawashe

'It's your fault,' the woman's silence screams at me. I bow my head and put my hands over my eyes because I do not want her to see that I totally agree.

#

I have always been told that it is my fault. I have not had the comfort of considering myself unfortunate, cursed, or bewitched. I have never found solace in the pew because the devil has not played any part in the hell that I have lived on this earth. Each time, I have just done it to myself. Every time something has gone wrong, there has been someone close by to remind me that it is my fault, just in case I forget. Now, I do not need anyone to tell me that it is my fault. Now, I know that I only have myself to blame for this mess that is my existence.

'It's your fault for making me this angry,' complained Ray after he had beaten me yet again. This time it was not for a missing button on his shirt or the call that a male colleague of mine had made to ask me to cover for him the next day as he had to attend a funeral. I had asked him why he came home at dawn. That set him off. 'I am not your poodle!' he yelled at me. 'I am a man. I have the right to come and go as I wish without a woman that I paid so much money for, dictating to me.'

Instead of keeping quiet then, I told him that I was not going to stand for his opening of his zipper whenever a woman passed by. That was when he gave me a bloody eye, a split lip, and several bruised ribs. Then he made me apologise for calling him a whore.

'It's your fault for not reporting that brute to the police,' my doctor told me as he examined another x-ray sheet to determine if Ray's kind of loving might have left internal souvenirs. The puffed eyes, cut lips, and countless bruises would soon fade away and I could discard the burqa and the oversized dark glasses. The doctor did not really say that but that is what he meant when he said, 'Maybe you should consider seeking help. Someday you may actually be maimed or even killed if this continues.'

But how could I shame myself, my husband and the whole family by washing our filthy bed linen in public? It was not as if Ray beat me up all the time; it had only happened about fifty times in three years. Anyway, most of the times it was just mere slaps. The real bad ones were only four really. And it was not as if he was a bad man. He was a good father and he often made me laugh. It was only his intense emotions that made him wary of other men's interest in me. Besides, it was not as if I had not known that he had a volatile temperament before I married him. It was his unpredictable nature that attracted me.

'You should not make me so angry. Why do you do this to me?' Ray always asked me plaintively after beating me. His sunny personality would soon emerge from the storm of his temper and I would not be able to resist the urge to put my arms around him and tell him that I would try harder. I kissed him in passionate forgiveness when the sight of my battered face raised the ghost of regret in his conscience. Or perhaps it was just shame that his friends and relatives would know that he had married a woman who had to be beaten repeatedly as she was just incapable of being a good wife. Why could I just not freeze our lives at those happy moments like when he would throw our little son up in the air while smiling tenderly at me? It was up to me to make sure that I did not enrage him so he wouldn't have to lay a hand on me. If I kept my stupid tongue in check instead of nagging him, he would be the most angelic of all men. So how could I go to the police and report when it was my fault? How could I stand the contempt of the police, men and women, as they accused me of infidelity or worse because a woman must have done something real bad to earn a beating? Even if Ray paid a fine, the whole world would know that I was a failure as a woman. I could not please my husband. So I ignored the doctor's advice and tried my best to be a better wife.

'It's your fault,' pointed out my mother when I eventually showed her my injuries. 'You should not challenge your husband like that. It is not even as if you caught him in the act with another woman. Anyway, no man is ever totally faithful. As long as he looks after you financially and does not do it in your face, just pretend not to see it and your life will be much happier.' I listened to my mother because she obviously knew what she was talking about; my father had never laid a hand on her, as far as I knew. I did not have the courage to tell her that this was not the first time. I turned a blind eye to Ray's numerous affairs. Even when they became blatant, I pretended not to know about them, and mother was right. On the surface we were quite happy, but inside, I was dying slowly every day.

Now that he had me submissive and totally pliant, Ray no longer needed to beat sense into me. At times I thought the mental torture of being a wife in name only was worse than the pain of a physical beating. At least then he had cared enough to react to my actions. Now he hardly noticed my existence and he was gone most of the time, sometimes for days on end on his endless 'business trips.'

'It's your fault,' Ray told me once again when I found out that he was keeping a woman in a flat. By that time she'd had his baby and he had also paid a handsome bride price for her without even having the courtesy of telling me or my parents about it. 'You are always going off to church. You do not take care of me. The maid does my laundry and cooks my food. If you could, I suppose you would let her even take your place in my bed. I need more from a wife. A real woman cooks for her husband and kneels too when she serves him. But you, oh, no, it is as if your legs were carved out of wood and if you bend your knees they would break.' I had learnt to keep a civil tongue in my mouth and did not say anything about the countless dinners that I had lovingly slaved over after a long day at the office and then fed to the dog because Ray had not come home.

But the spirit that he had trodden into the ground briefly raised its head at the injustice of it all. He was the one who now only occasionally visited the marital home. Had I not turned to prayer out of misery? To seek the strength to keep on carrying this heavy burden that had become my marriage? I walked out in anger.

'It's your fault,' Ray's sister told me when I went to tell her that Ray had taken a second wife. She already knew and did not bother to hide her preference for the latest model of servitude. 'You are obviously not enough of a woman for my brother. Otherwise he would not be forced to turn elsewhere for happiness.' She and the rest of his family made it clear that I could accept the situation gracefully or pack up and go.

But my dear mother would not hear of me leaving Ray. 'It will be your fault if your marriage breaks up. So he has married another woman, but has he asked you to leave? Is he no longer sleeping with you? Is he no longer looking after you?' All this she demanded in a voice that brooked no argument. So I humbly went back and lived with the bitter-sweet privilege of being second best in Ray's life. At least I still had a husband unlike those poor spinsters and divorcees who spent all their lives eyeing other women's men. I spent countless days and nights waiting for him to come home. Sometimes he did, and my life would be complete until he disappeared again.

Needless to say, I was not going to chase him away altogether by demanding that he ration his life more equitably between his two houses. But I made every effort to make mine the home that he would prefer. Scented sheets, impeccable personal hygiene and perfect meals were the hallmarks of the hotel that awaited his brief stays. My gym membership was no longer about keeping fit, rather it was about maintaining my looks for my husband. All the kitchen tips, I followed religiously, but somehow the other woman remained firmly in the picture. There were times when I fantasised about going over to her house to teach her a lesson. But I did not want to force my husband into disciplining me.

'Look at what Ray bought me for my birthday,' I would breathlessly gush to my workmates, to prove that in spite of what they whispered behind my back, my husband still loved me. I would not mention that the gift usually came after repeated prompting or that, at times, Ray did not even know of its existence.

'It's your fault,' my father-in-law declared as we gathered around Ray's deathbed. 'You have obviously bewitched my son because he preferred his second wife to you.' He embarrassed me in front of all the relatives who had gathered to see my husband breathe his last. And Ray took his sweet time about it too, lingering, way after the doctors had warned us that he was not long for this earth because he had left it too long and even the second-line drugs would not be able to redeem his ravaged organs.

My husband was not a pretty sight as Kaposi's sarcoma helped everything else devour the living carcass that HIV had created. I could not speak. I could not ask how I would even think of killing the man that I had stood by for so long. Had I not sacrificed my pride and everything else just for the right to remain his wife?

Even as they accused me of witchcraft, Ray's family was quite happy to let me look after him and clean up his mess as he lay there, helpless like a maggot. It was my hands that bathed him and washed his stinking clothes and his soiled bed linen. I looked at Ray's emaciated hands, now all bone and skin and useless. I wondered if their open palms had ever landed on his other wife's cover-girl features in blind fury as they had so often done on mine. His devoted second wife kept her precious hands for soothing our husband's fevered brow. All her energy was reserved for calling upon her darling Ray not to leave her as she would die, too. At the very end, the only way that I could lay a claim to my husband was by handling his stinking faeces and lavishing ointment on his flaking skin while he poured his affections on another woman. It was as if I was a living ghost who could be safely ignored. And in the end all he could say was to tell me to look after the kids. There was not even a single word of love, a hint of apology, anything to show that he acknowledged my services.

'It's your fault,' my best friend, Sarah, pointed out when the second wife got most of Ray's estate after his demise. Instead of immediately following him into the grave as she had repeatedly promised to in front of his family, she grabbed everything she could lay her manicured claws on. I would not let Sarah help me try to claim some of the estate back even when she assured me that the court would be sympathetic to my cause. I was just too tired.

'You should have insisted on a civil marriage when you got married. Educated as you are, you knew perfectly well that a customary union would leave you open to abuse. You should have refused to even move in with him without a marriage certificate in your hands,' Sarah advised me when it was already too late. How could I explain that when we got married I was so besotted that I would never have believed that my Prince Charming would turn into a poisonous frog? In the first flush of love, at only twenty-four, what did I know about the pain of being a woman? What did I know of abusive husbands, when I believed that my own father was a gentleman who treated my mother like a queen?

#

The woman's voice brings me back.

'It is not your fault,' she says again and this time I lift my head. The counsellor's face looms closer over the bare wooden table between us, her eyes distended into white orbs with black dots behind her spectacles as she absently caresses the pink manila folder encompassing my fate. In subconscious mime, I rub the smooth dull-red fake leather of the practical chair beside me which is filled with emptiness. I try to find the person hiding behind the layers of face powder that highlight the counsellor's skin blemishes. Is she really saying that I was not to blame for this?

The moment stretches into infinity. The bright posters on the pale green walls urging one to be positive about being negative mock me. A fly hovers in the air separating our eyes but the movement of its wings fail to add any sound to the void for an endless moment before she summons her best professional smile and asks me if I fully understood the implications of my test result, how it is just a health issue. I cry harder as her strength flows into me and then I understand. The room appears to be brighter as though someone has given me a new set of eyes and I can see my life better . . .

Yes, everything was my fault, but not in the way I had thought. It was my fault that I let Ray cow me into believing that I caused his abusive behaviour. I should have realised that he was a monster and I should have left him. It was not as if I was some helpless uneducated being, relying on him for financial support. It was my fault for begging to be allowed to exist on the crumbs of his affection. I should have demanded a man who loved me fully and not have given in to his emotional blackmail. I should have had the strength to realise that he was the one with a problem and not me. My biggest fault has been to let myself be a victim. By giving in, I let that brutal bully I married turn me from a happy and confident woman into a pathetic creature, eager to do anything for him, because he always made me feel that I was at fault. And it is definitely my fault that I am now spending the rest of my life fighting this destructive virus that is in my bone marrow and which courses and curses my whole body through my blood.

The very first time that Ray infected me with gonorrhoea I should have insisted on condoms or no sex. But I listened to him as he told me that I was his wife and not a prostitute. I should have realised that my mother belongs to another generation. I should have had the pride to stand up to Ray's relatives. I should have had the courage to leave Ray. Instead, I stayed in the hope that one day I would find the crock of gold at the end of the rainbow. I am handicapped now, facing the reality of two tablets daily, one in the morning and one in the evening without fail. I fantasize about what I would do to Ray if he was alive. I would pay thugs to give him a taste of his own medicine. I would arrange for him to find me in bed with one of his friends or maybe even his equally lecherous father. Or maybe a pot full of boiling oil. Then I pull my mind back from such a destructive path.

Ray is dead and hopefully rotting in hell, and I am alive. From today I will live, not just exist. In fact, straight from here, I am going to see Sarah. I believe I am going to enjoy the shock that will go through Ray's second wife when she realises that this doormat will no longer allow dirty feet to be wiped all over it. And after that meeting, I will go shopping. I need new clothes to replace these widow's weeds that envelop my frame, obscuring curves that still look good, even if I say so myself. I am not going to mourn Ray for a minute longer. I have wasted too many years on self-pity. I have a lot of happiness to catch up on, laughter to let out and smiles to flash. I have plenty of love to give and receive. His family and everyone else will not be too happy about that. But that is not my problem and definitely not my fault.

MAMA DEAREST

Lisa-Anne Julien

Mama must hate being old and sick. I imagine it's difficult to arouse intimidation from a horizontal, helpless position. Her eyes just hold a crazed look. As her dilated pupils invite me in and I am about to fall headlong into her gaze, I notice for the first time that her eyes are the colour of warm hazelnut. In the past, my own eyes would always lower just a fraction of a second before hers drank me in. Now I see how that left eyelid, heavy with a couple more folds of skin than its right counterpart, straddles her eye in a most graceless manner. I feel her vacant look wash over me and, despite my inner resolution, I tremble. Her thin white dress, scattered with yellow circles of varying sizes, exposes her bony knees, and her legs, thirsting for moisture, are at a perpetual thirty degree angle. This opening between her legs reveals an adult diaper, the source of the room's putrid smell.

I look at her face again. Her bottom jaw is lower than where it should be and so her mouth hangs in the shape of a small misshapen O. Together with the lunacy that envelopes the eyes, it is the perfect look of fear. Or is that me being too ambitious? I hover parallel over her body again. Five inches away from her face, able to decipher from her breath that she'd had rice pudding for dessert that afternoon, I am about to conclude that this woman is in fact very mad. But, just then, her eyes give an almost imperceptible squint and for the briefest of moments, her gaze flirts with recognition. 'Mama?' Then it's gone.

'She doesn't recognise anyone,' a voice says from behind me.

I spin around to see a nursing assistant, a stocky girl with an enormous bust and a low Afro. She is tying back the faded paisley-patterned drapes. As she opens the windows, the air inside the cheerless room relaxes just a little. A tatty Bible sits on a small table beside Mama's bed and a framed print of what appears to be the French countryside hangs over her. I don't even have to pass my fingers over the layer of dirt on the bedside lamp to know that it is there. There is a dankness emerging from below me, as though dew is choked beneath the faded red and blue flowers that still strive to adorn the worn carpet. No flowers. No plants. Hardly anything associated with life in this room.

'She's been like that for a while,' the nurse continues. 'I doubt she even knows you're here.'

Oh she knows I'm here.

'Pardon, what did you say?'

I have grown accustomed to filling the lonely spaces with conversations with myself, and so, occasionally, thought and speech exchange places.

'I'm Fiona,' I say, stretching out my hand, unable to get my mouth into much more than a taut line with the bottom lip stretched up to meet the top.

'I'm Angel. Is this your Mom?'

'Oh no,' I say quickly. I glance back at Mama. 'She really doesn't recognise anyone at all?'

'Well, it's hard to be certain about that since she doesn't speak anymore.'

I swallow slowly. I feel Angel watching me with curiosity and I know it's because my eyes are glistening. What hell muteness must be for someone like Mama. All her ammunition is packed in between those jaws.

'Does Phindi still come to visit?' I ask.

'Oh, you know Phindi? Yes, she comes. Without fail, three times a week.'

Phindile. The other daughter-in-law. That's how Mama used to describe her, usually with an upward tilt of the head and a smile. On the contrary, when Mama used that phrase to refer to me, the word 'other' often had a hollow sound to it, and her eyebrows rose in perfect synchronicity with the word's intonation.

It had been over a year since I unexpectedly ran into Phindi just outside the regional Home Affairs building in downtown Johannesburg. I had been walking with my eyes facing downwards as I tried to avoid the rubbish on the pavement like someone with an obsessive compulsive disorder, when a voice saying my name broke through my mental mutterings at the bureaucracy of South Africa's immigration system. Even before I looked up to take in how her powdery pink jersey hung loosely over a long denim skirt, and the way the white cotton douk pulled her eyes back, giving her a somewhat Oriental air, I knew who it was. 'Fiona?' Two syllables, sung in a sweet, lyrical tone that sent me reeling back to the deep green hills of Greytown, Kwa-Zulu Natal, a decade earlier.

'When did you get to Joburg?' I whispered in her ear as we embraced.

'Long story.' She rolled her eyes waved her hand, nearly hitting a clearly irate man leaving the Home Affairs building. 'How are you? It's been years!'

'I'm fine. Fine,' I said hurriedly. 'So how is the family?' She knew what I meant. Perhaps she even saw me holding my breath.

'We're fine. I had another boy, Jabulani, last year, and Ayanda just started grade two. Andile is, well, the same. Happier though, since his new job on the West Rand.'

She laughed. I let out my breath to feign a laugh. I waited.

'And, well, Mama is . . .' She moved me out of the way as a small boy pushed a wheelbarrow filled with toilet paper, soap bars and toothpaste and parked it in front of an elderly woman spreading an old blanket to set up her ground-level stall. 'Mama isn't well at all,' she finished.

Consolation prize, I thought. Not bad.

As we walked towards the taxi rank I learned that almost two years ago Mama suffered a stroke while putting laundry out to dry on the line at the back of the house. Phindi found her sprawled on the grass, arms entangled in the washing line, the whites covering her face and the colours still damp in the large brown tub. A litany of medical problems was soon discovered: high blood pressure, Angina, diabetes, and a chronic pneumonia that often kept Mama in hospital for weeks. Phindi's husband eventually suggested that Mama stay in a nursing home with round-the-clock care.

'Actually, I'm on my way to see her now. A nice place on Signal Road in Brixton.'

I had fallen silent, face-down, bo-jangling around the rubbish.

'Fiona,' Phindi said in a soft voice.

'Phindi, please, don't.'

Mercifully we arrived at the taxi rank and although my taxi was in the same direction as those going to Brixton I pretended to be going elsewhere.

'I have to meet someone at Museum Africa.'

'But we haven't even talked about you. What happened when you went back to your home?'

I promised to tell her the full story when we next got together. We exchanged numbers, embraced, and said goodbye.

#

Angel pulls a thin sheet over Mama, covers her up to the waist, and tucks the sheet tightly under the mattress. It fails to keep the stench at bay.

'The office is just around that corner—just shout if you need anything.' Mama's eyes bore into Angel's back as she leaves the room.

'She's gone, Mama,' I finally whisper. 'It's just me now.' I sit on the bed beside her frail hip and lean my weight on my right arm. I feel her lucidity creeping in with an eerie tangibility. I feel the sheet tighten under me. I look down to see her fingers in a slow-moving clench. She walks her index and middle fingers along the sheets, stopping only when she meets my own hand with its bulging veins and knuckles pointed upwards. Her little finger moves from side to side and inches forward until it finds its counterpart on my hand. She hooks her little finger around mine, the familiarity complete.

'What, are you sorry now?' I say, yanking my finger away, a little thrown by her touch and aware of her ability to manipulate. I blink with anger but it doesn't scare the tears away. They fall and expand into perfect circles onto the white sheet.

So many vivid details I have kept alive over the years—like the way Mama's hideous, brown corduroy skirt hung from her protruding belly that day she hissed to the neighbour, 'That kwerekwere, I don't even know if she has a mother.' She thought I was not within earshot (true, she never cared for my feelings, but even for Mama such a derogatory, albeit common term for a foreigner wouldn't be uttered to my face). Or the way she would pat my husband's shoulder and rub her palms along his muscles every time he sat down at her table for Sunday lunch, these caresses an indication that he shouldn't worry about my threats to go to the police. Or her skilful ability to always end up standing next to my good side, the side of my face that wasn't swollen, cut, or purple. Or the smell of the hair food she massaged into my scalp after she offered to shampoo it once we had eaten those Sunday lunches, opting to light only one candle in the bathroom and so reducing the chances of seeing the bruises on my neck and chest.

One crispy July morning I told Phindi that I had decided it was time to go back to my home. There were emotional ashes that the war had created and which I had refused to sift through until now. A few days later, I left without saying goodbye.

'And by the way, I did have a mother . . . I did.' The absorptive capacity of the thin sheets is barely able to keep up with my tears.

Mama's right hand, with its long, brittle, yellow nails, begins to claw up the side of my body. It traces the curve of my hips and for a second lingers on my waist, before inching towards my lower back. Then she touches it and I understand. She feels the six-inch scar across my back and caresses it, her rough skin scratching mine. Her touch makes me want to vomit.

'It's still there, Mama,' I whisper as I turn around to give her a good view of the grotesque rising of skin that snakes across my back, the result of a lone but powerful stroke of a sjambok one autumn night when my husband's drunken hands were too unfocused to do the job. 'It isn't going anywhere.' The tears stop.

Mama groans: a haunting sound from the depths of her belly. She groans again, deeper and louder this time.

'Why did you let it happen, Mama?' I hiss at her, slowly trailing my finger across her abdomen, up between her flaccid breasts, eventually letting it rest at the concave base of her neck. I watch her eyes scream as I trace her Adam's apple with my long red nail. 'You could have done something.' I am repulsed by the rubbery softness of her skin. 'Anything.'

I feel stronger now. I had only planned to confront her. But I realise that I enjoy the smell of fear that emanates from her. Her eyes attempt to pierce every pore of my face with their pleas of self-control. 'Why didn't you love me?' Both my thumbs pass lightly over the glands beneath the chin, the pulsation thunderous in the silence of that room. 'Why didn't you protect me?' My tears return, dropping onto her emaciated chest and running into her armpits. I shiver; my thumbs press down. It is so clear now. Soldiers. Fire. Machetes. Mama.

'Fiona.' Two syllables. Soft, lyrical. Warm breath at the back off my neck and strong hands travelling from my upper arms all the way down to my wrists. Phindi. My shivers increase. 'Fiona. Stop.'

I allow myself to be raised from the bed by Phindi, and as she leads me away, my teary eyes remain stuck to the red and blue flowers of the worn carpet. We reach the door just as Angel enters with some adult diapers and a roll of toilet paper. I crane my neck past Phindi's shoulder to catch what I know is my last-ever glimpse of Mama. Her eyes never leave me. But she is forced to abandon her gaze as Angel turns her over onto her side and, in a swift action, hikes her nightdress up to her waist and begins taking apart the diaper. The action reveals the rancid state of Mama's buttocks. It also exposes to my eyes the many grotesque risings of skin that snake across her back.

THE SILENT LAUGH

Olufunke Ogundimu

My grandparents and I live in a one-storey, faded brown house in the middle of Atanda Street, one of the many narrow, packed-mud streets that make up the rambling Agege Market. Baba is dozing in front of the house, his feet propped up on an overturned bucket. Mama is sitting on the balcony above him. Her thick arms are on the balcony's railing. Her nose is buried in the pages of The Alagborodun but she turns to Baba every few minutes. Young women who walk by our house at this time do so with their eyes fixed on the ground. They fear Mama's tongue. She believes her tongue shields their straying eyes from Baba, and so her eyes would follow them till they stumble and fall. Mama reads the newspaper as Baba soaks in his daily dose of sunlight. He has to be aired every day to rid him of his musty smell.

I am at Mama's feet. I have an ayo board on my laps. I'm playing against myself—my right hand against my left hand. Below us rusty zinc-roofed houses spread out in all directions. They lean towards each other, mud houses hidden under a layer of cement. You don't have to look hard to see mud bricks peeping through the cracked cement. I can hear Musa's grinders screeching in the distance: grinding peppers, spices, and seeds to powder. One of the grinders screeches louder as it tries to wear off its new blades. Carriers scurry around below the balcony like termites, carrying sacks of beans, rice, and garri across their shoulders. Their naked torsos shine with sweat.

Mama reads the captions aloud and then mumbles through each story. I hear the rustle of paper every time she turns a page. It is my right hand's turn to play. I share a handful of ayo seeds into the cups hewn into the board. I hear Mama gasp above me. I look up to see her draw the newspaper closer. Her eyes have grown large behind her glasses. She jumps off her chair and heads downstairs. I follow her. She waddles down the wooden stairs. 'My husband,' she pants as she gets to the door that opens onto the frontage. Baba's face turns towards her. It is wreathed with an almost toothless smile.

'I saw in The Alagborodun that government is paying pension arrears. Remember, you have not given me the money for the women harvest head-tie you promised,' Mama says. Baba raises his eyebrows, his smile disappears. He grunts. Baba's speech is slurred. He's recovering from a stroke. Nobody can make sense of his mumblings—not even Mama. And so he took matters into his own hands: he stopped talking.

Baba snatches the paper out Mama's hands, smoothes it on his laps. He grunts as he reads the story. When he finishes, he shakes his head, pointing at the same time to the paper.

'What is it, the headline?' Mama asks.

Baba shakes his head.

'Your head.'

Baba's eyes redden.

'You want me to get your medicine?'

Baba sighs.

'Your wallet?'

Baba stamps his foot on the ground and writes in the air with a forefinger. Mama rolls her eyes. 'The biro?' she says. 'It is upstairs.'

She wraps her blue wrapper around her wide hips and walks towards the staircase that leads to Baba's room. Baba's once-erect frame, now bent from the waist, shuffles after her. I follow behind them but veer off to the balcony to return to my game. It's my left hand's turn to play. I drop seeds into my right hand's cups and do my best to ignore Mama's roars to Baba's silent questions. 'Gbemi,' she finally calls out.

'Ma,' I reply. I jump up, overturning the ayo board. The smooth seeds scatter across the floor. I scramble in the direction of Mama's screams. Her voice at full blast raises the hairs on Baba's upper lip. 'Ma,' I say again. Grandma's hearing has its own will; it comes and goes. But her hearing is here now. She grabs my left ear and tugs it hard, twice.

'It is your father that is deaf. That skirt-chasing demon that killed my daughter.' I'm sure my father heard Mama's bellow wherever he was. I am sure her curses chase after him, too. I move away from her reach. My ear still rings.

'Your granbaba wants to send you to his friend.'

Baba is at his desk. He closes the exercise book in front of him. I don't know why he bothers to hide his written conversations with Mama from me. She reads everything out loud. I get to hear their full conversations. Everything except the letters he writes when Mama isn't near. His biro is in between his forefinger and middle finger. His thumb was cut off during his days as a blacksmith in the Nigeria Railway yard at Iddo. His award for long service is next to his colonial standard two school leaving testimonial and his baptismal certificate from the Salem African Church, Ebute Meta. They all hang in their frames from the plywood pelmet that runs round the sitting room.

He opens a fresh page and writes in capital letters: 'Your granmama is a rumourmonger. She talks too much.' He underlines what he wrote again and again until the blue ink line turns dark. I look at Mama under my eyelashes. Her eyes are blazing at him through her glasses. He pulls out a double sheet from the middle of the exercise book, places the paper in front of him, and tips it slowly to the left, then to the right, aligning it with the exercise book. Mama's lips pouts but the hiss does not escape. We watch as the lined paper catches Baba's cursive swirls and dips – his es bend over the line gobbling it up in its open mouth. He starts with our address in block and a date in the top left corner. Moving to the next line, he salutes his friend before starting the body of the letter on the next line. Drops of sweat appear on his bald head. In his letter I have counted two hithertos, three therefores, and lost count of wheretos.

Mama's lips are puckered. She shifts from one foot to the other. Baba flips over the paper and continues writing. He stops at the bottom of the page and ends the letter faithfully with his name and title, O.E. Babawande JP. After handing the letter to me, he opens the exercise book again and writes: 'Give the letter to my friend Pappy and bring back his reply.' He closes the book and tells me to go with his right hand but motions me with his left hand to come back.

Mama walks out of the room with me. Her nose is flared. She lets out the hiss—a loud one. 'Have you eaten lunch?' she asks. I shake my head no, avoiding her eyes because I had eaten some of the beans and corn pottage she cooked last night and then added a cup of water to the pot to make it up to the palm oil line near the rim of the pot.

'Don't mind your granbaba, he is too wise for himself. Go and ask his friend what serious people that are not rumour carriers read. Deliver your granbaba's letter. And don't stay out long, the sun is hot—fever sun. Come back quick-quick o!'

I wait for Mama to go to her room. I hear her door slam. As I walk by her door, I hear her talking to herself about head-ties and wrappers. I slip back into grandfather's room. He hands me one of his other letters and shoos me away. I run out of the house, my rubber slippers slapping the ground. The wind lifts my braids off my neck. I run through the haze of flies in the butchers' lane, turn left into the appliance lane where smoke-belching generators power music systems and television sets, and take another right turn which leads me to the alley that bursts into the Elewe omo lane. I walk slowly through the lane catching my breath. I look into the dark shops. Lining rickety shelves are clay pots, calabashes and bottles whose contents are known only to the herbalists selling them. Canopies block out the sun, locking in the smell of dried herbs and urine from caged animals. Red-headed lizards scramble about in cages, peering at tortoises, cats and rabbits in other cages. Piles of seeds, leaves, barks and roots pour out of rickety stalls; the stall doors are draped with animal skins and bones.

I walk out of the elewo omo lane into warm sunshine, past the telephone mast at Oguntade Junction—the same mast that blinks red at night from my bedroom window. I turn right to the Agege train stop and engine oil-covered stones crunch under my slippers. Beggars sit by the tracks under faded umbrellas surrounded by begging bowls and piles of coins. I walk along the line of rickety stalls that form a loose fence along the length of the track, trying hard to keep the market from spilling onto the railroad. I jump over timber sleepers lying across the tracks, occasionally over a pool of urine, a blob of sputum or a pile of shit.

Pappy's newspaper stand is a wide table that's covered with many different newspapers. It is beside a brand-new; 'No Loitering, No Parking, No Hawking, No Waiting' sign. From his stand I can see the beaded crown of the Oba of Agege's bronze statue. Its agbada folds molded in bronze drapes the huge standing body. Beside the newspaper stand is Mama Sunday's snack stand; a large charcoal fire licks the soot-covered bottom of the pan. The pan of boiling oil is filled with floating lumps of puff-puff. The aroma of frying batter competes with the stench of the nearby open gutter. I make sure Mama Sunday sees me. When she does she waves me over for my regular. She plops two fluffy puff-puff balls into an old newspaper. Hot oil soaks through the paper, rubbing off the ink.

'How is your granmama?'

'She's fine, ma.'

'Remind her of next Saturday's wedding. Tell her the colour of the day is gold and powder blue,' she says, stressing the word 'powder.'

'Please, ma, where is Pappy?'

She frowns at me and sighs. She bends down to check the batch of puff-puff turning golden brown in the oil, and turns them over with her long frying spoon. She stirs, but she's not looking at them, she's looking at me. 'Tell your grandma that she asked a cat to safeguard her meat. She has given her dinner to a cat to eat.'

'Don't understand, ma. We don't have a cat.'

She smiles. 'It is not for you to understand. Your granmama will. Tell her that the thing she worked for in the morning of her life is about to be stolen.' And she points to a group of people talking loudly to her left.

I spot Pappy in their midst. His brown kangol cap hides his small beady eyes. His deep voice can drown out a lot of voices but his small stature is easily swallowed in a crowd. He steps in to referee only when his customers' arguments are about to erupt into fights. His regulars discuss the papers—obituaries, editorials, sports, politics, job vacancies, everything. Pappy is Baba's friend; they both worked in the Nigerian Railway. Pappy started the newspaper business when he retired. 'I am retired but not tired,' is the name of his stand. I try to wriggle into the crowd but I can't get to him. An argument about Nigeria's defeat in the football world cup keeps the crowd restless and noisy. I wait till a spot near Pappy thins out. I put my hand into the crowd and tug at his buba. He sees me and shoulders his way out of the crowd. He pulls me to one side, close to the gutter. I can feel his potbelly outlined under his brown buba. I give him Baba's letters. He turns them over in his hands and lets out a loud cackle.

'How is my friend?'

'He's fine, sir.'

'Still not talking?'

'No, sir'

'And our wife?'

'Mama's fine too.'

I watch the vehicles along Oba Ogunji Road as Pappy reads the letters. The cars are crawling down the little bit of tar left by the pothole that has gobbled up most of the road. Street vendors weave in and out of the long stretch of traffic. Then Pappy tears a strip of plain paper from the large piece he uses to keep dust away from his unsold newspapers. He writes his reply to Baba on the paper fragment and then hands it to me with a fifty naira note. NIPOST stamp money, he tells me, and winks at me with both eyes. 'Tell your granbaba that the trap has not caught the rat yet, but the rat is sniffing at the bait.'

Baba and Mama are in the sitting room when I get back. Baba's old transistor radio is crackling on a side stool. He is tuning the radio. I give him Pappy's letter. He opens it and his eyes flick across the words.

'What does it say, my husband?'

Baba drops the letter on the stool and resumes tuning the radio between bands. He listens to snatches of broadcasts from stations all over the world. Finally he locks the dial on Radio Lagos. The radio crackles louder. He moves his ear nearer to the speaker and crosses the two antennae. We do not catch a news broadcast. He frowns and shoves the letter to Mama. She snatches it out of his hand and reads it. She takes her time. She hands it back to him. Then he shoves it at me, too. It reads, 'All the newspapers are silent on the matter, but word on the streets confirms payment of our arrears soon.'

I look at Baba frowning at the radio. Mama tries to keep her face straight but a smirk keeps slipping out. Mama turns to me and says, 'Don't mind your granbaba, he never listens to me.'

Baba's frown deepens. I've been trying to catch his eyes but he's still staring at the radio. I deliver Mama Sunday's message to Mama. Moving to Baba's side, I tell him Pappy's message. They look at each other. The radio crackles louder in the silence. Mama hisses. I look into her face. It is pinched. Her lips pout and slacken. I watch veins pop out in her neck. I cringe and move away from her. She shakes her head at me, closes her mouth with a snap, and points to a spot beside her. I sidle to the spot. She asks me to repeat what I just said. I do. She leans back in the chair and faces Baba.

'Do you have anything to say?'

He is silent.

'About this cat and rat business?'

He reaches for the radio but she grabs it first and flings it to the floor, where it sputters and dies. She takes hold of an exercise book and biro and shoves it under Baba's nose. Baba swipes both away like you would an annoying fly and, standing up from his chair, walks out of the room. I look at Mama and see that there are tears in her eyes. I watch them fall, washing off her tiro. Dark tracks run down her talc-powdered cheek—I remember my mother's tear-drenched face. I go to Mama's side and lift up my skirt. I wipe her tears off her cheeks with the end of my skirt, like I wiped tears off my mother's face after she fought with my father. I start to cry too. Mama pulls me between her thighs.

'What did I do, Mama?'

It's not your fault.'

She wipes at my tears with the edge of her wrapper. Then she swallows her sobs until her chest stops heaving.

'Stop crying,' she says. 'I have to go to Mama Sunday. I have to know the cat.'

#

Baba's cockerel, the one he's been fattening up for Christmas, didn't wake me up today. A woman's shrill cry did. I stumble out of bed, angry that I hadn't sunk my teeth into the juicy chicken thigh I was dreaming about. I hit my knee against the edge of a stool. I swallow my pain—I have to finish my house chores before Mama awakes. I limp to the window to get a better view of the woman whose cry woke me from sleep. It is Mama. She is at the end of our street. The cool morning wind carries her voice into my room.

'May she never know peace, the stupid woman that wants to marry my husband. I will cut off that thing of his, that thing he can't control, that thing that will not respect itself in old age. That woman's tongue will be eaten by dogs. Her liver and gallbladder will never give her peace. May her insides decay and be filled with maggots while she is still breathing. Leave the husband of my youth alone.'

I hear Baba open his door. He walks to the toilet. He returns to his bedroom, his left foot is dragging louder than usual. I hear him pace around in his room. I go back to my bed. I lift up a side of my mattress to pick up an envelope. I open its flap and remove a picture. Its left side is jagged. Mama tore away the other half—my father. She said it was a sin to keep a demon in the house.

I look closely at a woman laughing with all of her face. I can see Baba and Mama in my mother's face. Mama's full lips and dimples, Baba's arching eyebrows and cleft chin. I put the picture close to my ears and try to hear that silent laugh caught in the picture. It has drowned out a lot of voices and questions in my life. I hold it up against my ear. Maybe her laughter can drown out Mama's angry voice, too.

THE AMERICAN

Mercy Dhliwayo

Her mother was unforgiving. She did not take public humiliation lightly. She had not been promised anything really. However, having heard so much about her potential son in-law, including that he was not only white but also an American, an American was what she expected and an American was what she had promised the few friends and family members she invited for lunch on that special Sunday. Each friend had been invited for a reason. Mai Ruva because her daughter was getting married to a doctor, Mai Nyambo because her two daughters were based in England, Mai Gonzo because she thought she was better than everyone else in Mufakose, and the rest just so they could see how well her family was doing. Chenje, however, had not seen the reason for all this. This was not a marriage ceremony, after all. She was merely introducing her boyfriend to her parents. She thus would have been happy with just a small, intimate family lunch, but her mother was not one to show off small.

There was only one car that Chenje knew to make such grumbling noises when it approached, and that car was her arch-rival, Thandiwe. Everyone who knew the car could identify her approaching from a distance. Chenje did not hate Thandiwe because Antonio paid too much attention to her. She hated her because the old scrap embarrassed her. Antonio took it everywhere they went, the mall, exhibition openings, award ceremonies, and even ministerial gala dinners. Among the X5s and other luxury cars, there she would be, an old 1954 Chevrolet Bel Air, covered in dust accumulated from a weekend at a game reserve or any other out-of-town trip. Always the odd one out. Yet Thandiwe was Antonio's darling, his sweetheart, his source of pride. He did not seem to understand that the likes of Thandiwe were only okay for their artsy friends, the free-spirited types that marvelled at the beauty of nature and crawling insects. That type, who perceived beauty in the most obscure things, would not mind Thandiwe at all. But Chenje's family was not that type.

Chenje rushed out of the house to investigate the approaching sounds, and sure enough, there she was. Thandiwe- injury number one- heading towards Chenje's parents' yard, noisily as though summoning a revolution.

Boiling with anger, Chenje rushed forward to meet the car before it made it to the gate. Thandiwe slowed down.

Chenje bent forward and stuck her head through the driver's window and said, while concealing her anger, 'Sweetie, I thought we agreed that you guys would use James' car.'

'James' car had no gas, love, and mine has a full tank. So it made more sense to come with Thandiwe instead of pouring gas into another car.'

Chenje shot an angry look at James who sat in the passenger's seat.

'Sha, you know this man of yours is stingy,' James responded to her look in Shona. Contrary to James' utterance, Chenje found Antonio too generous. Always rushing to pay for the next round of beer and lending friends money that never came back. He probably had not poured fuel in James' car because of the warnings she had given him about friends like James; the type that never took out their wallets when they went out.

'Saka, you failed to pour a little bit of petrol in your car to get here? Did you think I would not pay you if you wanted payment? You even failed to tell him to wear something decent. Some kind of friend you are,' Chenje said, also responding in Shona. She scowled at the clothes Antonio wore: Injury number two. Did he really get a kick out of embarrassing her? He wore his faded blue track pants with 'New York City' printed downwards on the left leg and that school uniform-like khaki shirt with little prints of the marijuana plant all over as well as a portrait of Marcus Garvey on the front. His hair, as usual, was uncombed, and was thus beginning to entangle into locks. Had Antonio no intention of marrying her which would better her chances of getting a green card in America where she intended to live her life, she would not have kept him around this long, for no self-loving woman deserved such humiliation.

Antonio, feeling left out on account of the language barrier, gazed at Chenje, seeking meaning in her words. The flaring of her noise and squinting of her eyes told him that she was angry. 'What has James done now, my love?' he said to her. 'Come on, smile for me. It is a beautiful day. I'm finally meeting your parents.'

'Yes you are, Tony. And I assume you did not see the clothes I ironed for you this morning.'

'What is wrong with what I'm wearing? You're too uptight sometimes, Che. Here, this should cheer you up.' Antonio reached for a stuffed teddy bear displayed on the dashboard of his car, and handing it to Chenje, he said, 'Meet Teddy. Isn't she adorable? When I saw her she reminded me of you. Sweet and tender.'

Grabbing the teddy bear from Antonio, Chenje ordered him and James to go and wait for her at a nearby shopping centre until she found him something decent to wear. Antonio protested at this. He did not like it when Chenje tried to control his appearance, but at this point, his dislikes did not matter. Without entertaining his protest, Chenje walked away from Thandiwe and disappeared into her parents' yard. Having found some clothes in her brother's room that she deemed suitable, Chenje folded them into a paper bag and once again left the house.

The family had begun arriving. When Chenje got to the gate with the bag of clothes for Antonio, her brother, Raymond, had arrived with their aunt, Auntie Rhoda, whom he had gone to collect in their father's Volvo. To Chenje's dismay, Thandiwe, despite her instructions, was parked beside the Volvo. She could see Auntie Rhoda scrutinizing Thandiwe from front to back and top to bottom, and even peeping inside. At that point, James got out of the car and extended his greetings to Auntie Rhoda. Antonio followed suit. Raymond, who was already acquainted with both men, introduced them to his aunt.

'Oh, so this is the American?' No one responded to the Auntie Rhoda's remark. Chenje could see her disapproving eyes moving from Antonio's shirt to his track pants and the old leather sandals he wore. Chenje shyly extended her greetings to her aunt and then led her into the house, followed by the trio.

The excitement in the house at Antonio's visit seemed to disappear on his arrival. His presence summoned aloofness in Chenje's family and more especially in her mother, whose vivacious and conversational self appeared to have been overthrown by a cloud of humiliation that became more prominent as her friends arrived. Auntie Rhoda's presence worsened the situation. She was known for her 'cash talk' and it did not take her long to unleash it. This she did shortly after formal introductions had been made and in the presence of everyone without the courtesy of speaking to Chenje privately. She had at least been courteous enough to speak in a language Antonio did not understand.

'Seriously, my child, is this what you have brought for us? Did we not send you to school? What has made you so naive so as to believe the foolish lies boys tell you on the streets? What American is this? Can you say this is an American wearing pata-patas from Bata? This one here who looks like a white boy you just picked up from the streets? Even the boys who sell tomatoes at the terminus dress better than this!'

Chenje's father, maintaining the language code, came to his daughter's rescue. 'Sister, behave yourself. This is not the way to talk in front of guests.'

Auntie Rhoda, ignoring her younger brother, turned her attention to Antonio and said, 'So what is it that you do for a living?'

'I am an artist.'

'An artist? Is there money in drawing people?'

Antonio chuckled. 'I do not draw people'

'So what do you draw? Animals and hills?'

'He does not draw, Auntie. He is a musician,' Raymond said, laughing.

'Oh, a musician.' Auntie Rhoda was quiet for a while, and then said, while scrutinizing Antonio's sandals:

'But you look nothing like the musicians we see on TV. Exactly what type of music do you sing?'

'A fusion of jazz and alternative music.'

'Really. It's a pity though. Most musicians are very promiscuous. Many of them are dying so young.'

Chenje's mother stood up abruptly, and after clearing her throat, she asked Chenje to help her in the kitchen. Her father at that point also stepped in. 'How are you finding Zimbabwe?'

'It is a beautiful country, I must say. The people here are warm and welcoming. It's different from Cincinnati. I love it here.'

'So why did you come to Africa?' This was Auntie Rhoda at it again.

'To explore its beauty. There is so much beauty here that people do not seem to recognize.'

'Oh, I see. So when you are done exploring, what are your plans with our daughter?'

'We have spoken about marriage and that is something we are thinking of.'

'So if you marry our daughter, where will you two be living? Surely not at our daughter's little flat.'

'We actually have bigger plans. We want to buy a farm. If all goes well we should have a farm within the next two months.'

Upon hearing this statement from Antonio, Chenje walking out of the kitchen, dropped the plate she was holding. 'He is not serious, is he?' she exclaimed to no one in particular.

After Antonio's mention of the farm, the aloofness of the family seemed to disappear, and everyone now conversed with him as if he were an old friend. They spoke of him with pride.

'You see, white people are down to earth,' Chenje's father said. 'They do not need to show off their wealth like you black people.'

'You are right, Brother.' Even Auntie Rhoda had softened up. 'After all, the white people do say, do not judge a book by its cover. Did you see the groceries he brought? Brown rice, olive oil, organic chicken. Quality only.'

To Chenje's mother, it did not matter what he had brought. Her ego had been bruised. This was not what she had promised her friends. She had seen them casting looks at Antonio and then exchanging talking eyes amongst themselves. She said to her daughter, 'You could at least have prepared him some decent clothes. Can you imagine what my friends are saying right now? And that crazy aunt of yours. Can she never shut up? It's like you all conspired to humiliate me in front of my friends.'

'I did not ask you to invite any of those people, Mother. You brought this upon yourself.'

'Oh, so it's my fault! I raised you better. Was I wrong to expect better? Whoever goes to visit his potential in-laws wearing ma'pata-pata. Is that the American way?'

'That is how he is, Mother,' Chenje said with finality. 'Deal with it.'

#

Later that evening, when they arrived at their apartment, Chenje questioned Antonio about the farm. It was then that Chenje realised how serious he was about buying the farm he had been talking about for the past week. She had often heard him speak about wanting to own his own piece of land, but like any of his fantasies about a perfect world with no hunger or war, Chenje had never taken it seriously. It now sunk in. Not only was he serious about the farm, he was actually serious about settling in Zimbabwe. He had no plans of returning to America. Not even on that 'one day' that she had hoped would come soon. Her one-way ticket to America had vanished into thin air. The ultimate injury.

Chenje could not hide her disappointment. 'But we didn't agree on this, Toni?'

'I didn't know there was anything to agree on? I thought we both wanted this.'

'This is not exactly what I want at this point in my life. You know I have always wanted to get out of here and go someplace where I can actually put my degree into use and also get my career on track. And I thought that we were going to try this together in the States. How will we do that if we get this farm and settle here? We can do the whole farm thing later in life. Can't we just focus on our careers right now?'

'But, love, there is no reason why we cannot focus on our careers from here. Besides, you have never been to the States. How do you know that what you are looking for is out there?'

'I do not need to have been there to know that things are a lot better than here. Anyone can see how better my cousin's life has been since she left. Everyone can see how better off her family is doing now. Why can't I have that?'

'You already have so much here. Perhaps you need to stop comparing yourself to everyone and just be content with what you have. This is where I wanna be. I am happy and free here.'

'Oh Tony, please stop. Why won't you open your eyes? There is nothing here for you. And there is certainly nothing here for me. I mean, everyone is leaving Zimbabwe for greener pastures. No one in Zimbabwe or Africa wants to lead a simple life gazing at the beauty of the moon, marvelling at insects, or walking around barefoot in the thorny and bushy landscapes of "beautiful Africa." We already have thousands of kids walking thousands of miles barefoot to school. We do not want a simple life. We want shoes. We want a decent life. We want decent jobs and decent salaries that can allow us to save for the future. I want all of that and, most importantly, I want to get out of this place.'

'Then perhaps you are with the wrong man, Chenje. Like I said, this is where I want to be. And I will do all I can to get that farm. With or without your help.'

Chenje had never heard Antonio sound this stern. She often wished that he would have a backbone instead of always being too nice and too gentle. Any other time his sternness would have turned her on, but at this moment, it confused her. Even angered her. Overwhelmed with emotion, Chenje stormed out of the apartment and found herself heading straight towards Thandiwe. She got into the driver's seat and picked up the teddy bear from the passenger's seat where she had left it earlier after Antonio had given it to her. She pressed the teddy bear against her chest and began sobbing. She had invested three years in their relationship yet she was still in Zimbabwe and had nothing to show for it. What then had been the purpose of their relationship? Although being Antonio's girlfriend had its own benefits, such as not having to pay her own rent or to buy groceries, she wanted more in life. She had not left her job just to become her boyfriend's concert manager and to follow him around to every performance. And she was tired of being constantly spotted going in and out of Thandiwe and the embarrassment that came with it. She had expected that, at this point in her life, she would be an employed economist living a proper and fulfilling life in Cincinnati or maybe Chicago or even LA. Yet here she was, about to spend the rest of her life on a damned farm in some rural part of Zimbabwe, her life just wasting away. When she had cried all that she could, Chenje gazed at the teddy bear for a long time, and then she finally smiled. 'Sweet little Teddy,' she whispered before she kissed it on its woolly head. She then got out of the car, leaving Teddy behind.

#

No amount of time could make Chenje reconcile with Antonio's decision. Almost two months had elapsed since the Sunday lunch with her family, and during that period Antonio, on the one hand, had finalised a sale agreement for the farm and had already paid fifty percent of the purchase price. All that was left was for him to pay the remainder and claim his farm. He had thus sold shares he owned in one of his father's companies and the money had just been transferred into Chenje's bank account, which he had been using for years. Chenje, on the other hand, had had time to think about what she wanted to do with her life. After much deliberation, she had resolved that she was not going to be some farm girl or farmer's wife and that she did not need Antonio to follow her dreams. She was going to America on her own and she was not going to waste any more time than she had already wasted in waiting for Antonio. It had taken her a month to plan her departure and her time to leave had finally arrived, and she had not told Antonio anything about it.

Sitting at a table with Antonio, James, and her brother, all of whom she had met for an early lunch, Chenje recalled her brother's reaction when he learnt of her plans to leave. He had found her plans too rushed and had tried to persuade her not to leave.

'You should at least tell Antonio. He deserves to know. You owe him that,' he had said.

'I do not owe him anything. He made his decision and since he really wants to settle in Zimbabwe, I am going to give him a real Zimbabwean welcome. And he is damned if he thinks he is going to get his citizenship through me.'

'Calm down, Sis. What's with the anger?'

It had surprised Chenje that her brother had detected the anger she harboured within, when even Antonio, who was obsessed with the spirituality and celestial energies, had failed to sense what was happening with her. She had ensured that after their altercation over the farm business, they made up the following day and life returned to 'normal.' Antonio reverted to his usual jovial self, oblivious to the anger growing within the woman he woke up in bed with and made love to every day.

Antonio sat across from her on the table, and he was brainstorming with James and Raymond about what they were going to do with the farm: the rooms they were going to turn into studios and guestrooms, the fresh vegetables they were going to produce, the orchard and the many varieties of herbs they would have. 'Perhaps we could even have a little secret herb garden, too,' James said, referring to a marijuana garden.

'Maybe we should place our orders now,' Chenje interrupted. She hated the carelessness with which they spoke about marijuana. This was Zimbabwe. To Antonio, however, Zimbabwe, and Africa in general, was some sort of heaven where everything was irie. And this stupid notion had rubbed off on his friends, or at least, the idiotic ones like James. They had even already purchased some marijuana the previous day in Binga. Chenje had strongly disapproved of them travelling with it back to Harare, especially with all the roadblocks that had been set up across the country in light of the festive season. However, with friends like James, who, as usual, had tagged along on their spontaneous two-day outing, there was no reasoning with Antonio.

'Come on, Chenje. Stop being so controlling,' James had said in a bickering tone. 'I will personally take care of it. So don't worry. I will hide it in the least suspicious place.'

With a growing hatred for James, Chenje had distanced herself from their plans. She wanted no part of it. She did not even want to know where they hid it. She, after all, had plans of her own to worry about.

Everyone now placed their orders. Antonio ordered a veggie stir fry, Raymond a plate of sadza and some steak, while James ordered the priciest meal, a rack of ribs with Buffalo wings. Chenje's order stunned the table: a flame-grilled rump served with a baked potato. 'Make sure the steak is well done, but not dry,' she said to the waitress.

'Are you sure?' a confused Antonio asked.

'Yep.' Chenje took a large sip of her cocktail, unbothered by the eyes staring at her. When her order came, she sliced into her steak with a glorious smile on her face, and slid the chunk of meat into her mouth. When Antonio, with a confused and somewhat resentful glance, asked her about her sudden change in diet, she merely responded: 'I just felt like something different.' In response to this, Antonio asked her if everything was okay.

'Everything is perfectly fine, love. What could possibly be wrong?' Antonio did not say anything further. Neither did Raymond. James, on the other hand, burst into laughter.

'I thought being a vegetarian made you more spiritual and brought you closer to . . . what was that, oh, our true nature.' Chenje ignored James and continued enjoying her meal. She remembered saying things like that when she first became a vegetarian, but those were not her words. Those were Antonio's words. According to him, to get closer to God, one had to respect and preserve the life of all creatures, great and small. They had a right to life just as humans did. Such bullshit, Chenje now said to herself with a secret grin. Even the purest Jesus broke two pieces of meat and shared it with millions. Or was it fish? Same difference. Flesh was flesh whether white or red, and, right now, she wanted hers red. After over two years of being a vegetarian, she had accumulated a hunger for meat. She hungered for it just as she hungered for what she had been promised. Okay, not promised as such, but what she had expected of her relationship with Antonio. She would no longer suppress her hunger. There was, after all, no hunger in Zimbabwe. At least not in her part of Zimbabwe. The grocery stores that had sprung up at every corner in the city centre were packed with foodstuff and the butcheries were red with fresh meat. So who was she to deprive herself of such delicacies in a country that had begun to starve the western media of its favourite reports of empty food stalls and starving people?

After their awkward lunch, Antonio left with James and Chenje left with her brother. Before parting ways, Antonio reminded Chenje of their meeting at the bank later that afternoon for the transfer of the remaining payment on the farm. Chenje assured him that she would be there on time. She smiled as Antonio kissed her on her forehead and said see you shortly. She still felt the touch of his soft lips after he left. That was one thing she would miss.

'You can still change your mind, you know,' Raymond said as they walked to the car. He had noticed the distant look on Chenje's face.

'Just drive. My mind is made up,' she responded.

Raymond drove off as instructed. In about thirty minutes arrived at the airport, where Chenje was scheduled to catch a flight to China. She planned on staying there while she awaited the processing of her American visa application and thereafter leave for America as soon as her visa was processed. She had a Zimbabwean friend in China who had a friend at the US Embassy. Her friend had assured her that he would help her get her visa from China.

When she was ready to board her flight, Chenje embraced her brother for longer than usual, as though seeking assurance in his embrace that everything was going to work out. In that moment, Chenje found herself worrying about the possibility of Antonio having uncovered her plan and catching up with her before she took off. She wondered if Antonio had indeed not suspected anything about her departure and if he was really expecting to see her later that afternoon at the bank. He had not shown any suspicion. She had been discreet about everything. She had packed her travelling bag and removed it from the apartment in Antonio's absence. All she had taken from the apartment that morning were her handbag and Teddy, whom she had thrown into the handbag at the last minute, just as a souvenir. She had seen Teddy lying on the couch and staring at her that morning, and the teddy bear reminded her of the early days of her relationship with Antonio, when everything was still so exciting. When there was so much promise in Antonio, and when being with him had given rise to her American dream. She was now about to pursue that dream alone. And yet she could not stop worrying.

Raymond, too, was worried. 'Are you sure you have enough money?' he asked. 'I can give you that money that you paid me back, if you need it.' Despite assuring him that she had enough money, Chenje could still sense Raymond's concern, but she could not explain to him why he had no reason to worry about her finances. She released him from her grip and kissed him on the cheek.

'I will call you when I land.'

'And Tony?'

'I will call him too,' Chenje said despite having no such intentions.

'What do I tell him in the meantime if he calls looking for you?'

Chenje thought about it. She knew many questions awaited her brother after she was gone. She wished she had not involved him in her plans. She would not have told him anything if he hadn't refused to lend her the money she needed to purchase her plane ticket.

'Tell him we parted after lunch, nothing else,' she said.

'I don't understand why you couldn't be open with him.'

'You wouldn't understand, Ray. I have to go.'

As Chenje walked away from her brother, she thought about how much he did not understand. He did not know the real circumstances of her departure. He did not even know that the money she had paid him back had not come from Antonio to start any business venture she desired (as she had told her brother) but from the sale of Antonio's shares meant to pay the balance for the farm that afternoon. He did not know that she had not only used that money to repay what she borrowed from him, but that she had actually withdrawn all of it and deposited into a new account she had secretly opened, thus leaving Antonio with nothing but a VISA card to an account that had less than one hundred dollars. But Raymond was better off not knowing the truth.

It was only after Chenje had boarded the plane and was off Zimbabwean soil that she stopped worrying. After hours of flying, she finally landed in China. Grateful that she had made it, she walked with much excitement towards the security checkpoint. She thought of Antonio and his reaction to discovering that she had left the country and, the cherry on top, his reaction to discovering the balance in their account. She had no regrets whatsoever. The idiot had after all wasted three years of her life. Chenje passed through the metal detectors and waited for her handbag as it went through the scanner. Then the scanner beeped. The security personnel picked up the bag and replaced it on the scanner belt. Again the scanner beeped. Chenje could see the security personnel studying the scanner screen, and she wondered what the problem could be. Chenje's worry grew when one of the security officials asked her to step aside and handed the handbag to her with the instructions to empty its contents. Chenje bit her lower lip as she considered the possibility of her wrongs having been detected by the scanner. She considered what was in her bag. Apart from the VISA card for her new account, there was no evidence of what she had done. Perhaps Antonio had already discovered the withdrawal and tracked her down to China. But how would he prove that she had stolen his money? The money was in her account after all and was as good as hers. Chenje relaxed and proceeded to do as she was told.

Having emptied the contents of her handbag, the security official picked up Teddy and asked what was inside her. 'Nothing,' Chenje said, puzzled by this question. The official said something in Chinese to another official standing next to him. The second official then disappeared briefly and then returned with a pair of scissors. Chenje was horrified as the official, without any explanation, ripped open Teddy's belly. She was even more horrified at the sight of what fell out of

Teddy's belly. A package that did not take her any time to recognise: a sealed one-kilogram package of marijuana. Chenje was speechless. Her body went weak as she felt a cold pair of handcuffs shackling her wrists. This action was accompanied by the words: 'You are under arrest.' The other words that followed were drowned out by the sound of James's voice in her head: 'So don't worry. I will hide it in the least suspicious place.'

HAPPINESS

Bolaji Odofin

My cat has nine lives. I borrowed one, didn't return it, and she wouldn't let me have any more. A life is more useful to a cat than a Mhan, Todoma says, for a cat instinctively knows the soft, secret part of the anatomy of existence and a Mhan does not. We live, says she, Mhan merely is.

The day was overcast as I made my way to the office. It was in the upscale Cerulean underground, which has clean lines and transparent walls of the highest quality. Todoma had left for the university hours earlier. Under her supervision, graduate students split tiny matter. It was an old enterprise, finding the indivisible. Vekms, farls, quipps, mmorts, erwetzs and calem-8s enjoyed fame only for the interval it took to rend them apart. Todoma often lamented the thing's perversity. A garu she called it, a wikenwiti, Lentishe words for 'ghost' or 'wraith'. You could tell from the way her whiskers twitched when she said this that she would have it no other way.

'Good morning,' piped Nwa, my cheerful assistant. Living, breathing assistants were expensive anachronisms, but worth every kobbo.

'Morning, Nwa.'

She brought me hot pergolat, and I luxuriated in its spicy smell till it was time to make my rounds. Some of my patients were already restless. They were in transparent-walled rooms, their heads fitted with bubble-vision for their entertainment, should they want any. They often didn't. I examined Amikhe, a cat in his thirties, diagnosed with juggur, a genetically inheritable mental disease in which the patient experienced the presence of a 'twin' fused to his back, feeling the physical pressure of the visitor's perpetual motion as it 'pushed against some hard place, thon. He's wearing me out.' Bandewe was a vheectoloric feline with that disease's inability to see in the dark, a rash that spread from jaw to tail, and uncontrollable chatter. Inkushidi moaned constantly. Her right side was rigid, and her left paw viciously clawed the air in disjointed loops. At moments, without any warning, she would burst into wild violence and spittle-spattering hissing. Restraints didn't work. Vacuum Isolation did. Homme Uluku's pupils were contracted to soft black points, the symptom of his theyeria, a degenerative, incurable mythical disease that altered his personality and made him extremely dangerous. Having just woken up from sleep, he contemplated me with bleary-eyed amusement. 'What's up?'

'How are you feeling today, Homme?'

'Can't complain. Actually, I can. I want out. I'm fine. You can tell, can't you?'

'I don't think you're ready for that yet.'

'What do you know about it? Fafel little bastard.' He thrust his face forward and issued a threatening growl, but his heart wasn't in it. He yawned and turned his attention to my hand. I put it in my coat. Homme looked me in the eye and grinned outright. 'Thon, I'd pay attention to that hand of yours if I were you.' He rarely used my name, preferring instead the patronising Lentishe slang for Mhan. He turned away and switched on his bubble-vision. I was dismissed.

When my rounds were done, I made for the dimly lit pharmalog and burrowed in its gloom. Something, a feeling that was not a feeling, rose in the back of my throat and filled it with the taste of bitter things. I turned on the micro-transmitter behind my ear by thinking about it and sent Todoma a message: I don't feel fresh.

She responded immediately: Why?

I answered with a lie: I don't know.

I'd never lied to her before. I was momentarily distracted by this. But if she sensed it she made nothing of it. Let's go out, she said. We'll chase your sadness. We'll follow it like spies and see where it goes.

Cheering up a little, I told her: Yes.

I made my way back to my office.

Todoma.

I had no idea what it all meant, but whatever shades of meaning existed, she made life yield it. Fifteen years together. Sometimes it seemed like fifteen minutes, sometimes an eternity: like it had always been and would always be this way. It was hard to remember what life was like before we met, before she became the glue that held everything together.

I remember the day I first saw her as if it were yesterday.

I was late for the hospital where I was earning my MediPro license in psychiatry, and I'd hurried past a group of protesters outside a government building. They were transmitting loud protests that could be received half a mile in any direction. I got a headache and cursed as fluently as I knew how. Then a shout registered, as did what they were protesting about. A corporation peddling mental communications ware had subjected dozens of Mhan to illegal cognitive experiments. It was a huge conglomerate with subterranean offices in half the cities on Thukkur and a presence on several other planets. Specie-ist slurs from even the lowest creatures were daily directed at Mhan—many were those who wouldn't have you next to them in public places, who rejected your expertise and spurned your medical attention as soon as they saw what you were. Some were a little more subtle in their distaste: nodding politely in imitation acceptance and then retreating, tail between their legs, to one of their own for a 'real' consultation. But unlicensed experiments on involuntary subjects? My steps slowed indignantly.

I spotted a few cats among the protesters, and my eyes were narrowing at this when they encountered an extraordinary brown gaze. All my breath seemed to escape from me in a single whoosh, and I sagged like one of those squeaky half-liquid toys of my childhood. She was tall for a feline, fully six feet, with glossy black hair that shone with health. I don't recall other details well, so mesmerized was I, that everything else was blocked out and brown only there was in the world entire. We must have stood there like dummies for a while because she gave an abrupt shake of her tail as if to release herself from some enchantment. And then the police came and she was lost in the ensuing chaos.

Weeks passed while I went around the hospital like an automaton, voices and faces seeming to come at me in a kind of dream tinged with brown, now looming and loud, now receded and quiet. Unsuspected energies coursed through me, riotous and overpowering, and at the same time there was a river of calm, so that I was poised on a sort of ledge, intricately balanced. And then one day, while on an errand for Professor Kuku in the bustling Jopper area with its rows of floating shops and slant-eyed North Thukkur storekeepers, I ran into her. She had company - bright, vivacious things I noticed peripherally. Neither of us stopped, but as she passed I transmitted a number to her and hers came at me fast, but it was garbled. So hurriedly were the numbers dispatched. Sometime later, I saw her go by in a hoverbus, but there was no time to do anything but register her startled expression.

I did not see her again for a while. Gradually the perpetual knot in my gut eased, and I could concentrate on matters again. I was allowed a week off from the hospital to prepare for graduation, after which I would officially begin to practice as a MediPro. I decided to go on a picnic. That day the air was crisp, the skies tinged with red, and fallen leaves eloped with the wind. I sat on a bench in a hovering park and ate my esknya and drank my pergolat. I was hooking purple fingergrass between my toes when she dropped to the ground beside me. There was no surprise, only a sort of inevitability about the moment. We exchanged glances, but said nothing. After a while, I reached out a little shyly and took her hand. Then we leaned against each other and watched the world.

The talkathons came later, and the thing, almost a physical illness, that took us in its feverish arms whenever we were apart. She met my family, Ma, Da, Dug, Khale, and Crazy Uncle Musriil, and I was gratified by the ease with which they took to each other.

Todoma's parents were wealthy. Her father was a MediPro like me, specialising in general medicine, but most of the money came from her mother, who'd inherited it. They invited me to dinner one evening, during which I tried to ingratiate myself. Exhausted by the effort, I wandered out into the backyard, a garden with rare blue rock and filerrium fountains that must have cost a fortune. Todoma joined me. She pulled faces and swaggered about in imitation of famous people. We were giggling like juveniles when we heard her father clear his throat. Her parents had come into the garden. They smiled at Todoma, and then regarded me gravely.

'You're from the East, aren't you?' her mother asked, looking pointedly at my dusky skin and crinkly dark hair.

I returned her gaze levelly. 'What gave me away?'

'Be nice,' Todoma hissed at me in a low voice.

'You're Mhan, she's Lentishe,' her mother said.

Todoma nodded solemnly. 'What amazing eyesight you have, amyah.'

Her father watched her in silence for a few seconds before he said: 'Have you considered Claws?' I felt a sudden chill. 'Claws,' he continued quietly. 'Incurable. Fatal.'

Todoma went to him. She curled her tail around his legs affectionately. 'Aba-aah,' she said, drawing out the Lentishe word for father. 'How many bi-specie couples or quartets do you know with Claws? It's extremely rare.'

He was looking at me. 'You're merely crippled by it,' he said. 'But she dies. I take it this is fine by you? If she, er, relates within her own species she wouldn't be in danger, and neither will you, if you stick to yours. I take it both of you are already . . .'

Todoma cut in. 'That's none of your business, Abah. Really!'

Her father's eyes, a steely gray flecked with orange, held mine. 'Well?'

'I've thought about it,' I said slowly. Of course I'd thought about it! Sometimes it was all I could think about, though the statistical chances of contracting the disease were so low as to be almost nonexistent. Whenever I brought up the topic Todoma would laugh off my fears, and I would try to reassure myself with numbers. 'She's my life,' I told her father.

'You have yours,' he said.

Her mother snapped, "The disease doesn't care whose life it is, it'll take it anyway."

'Look, just stop it,' Todoma said irritably. 'You're being ridiculous. And I still have nine Replicas. Nine lives.'

Her mother looked shocked. 'A Replica is not a life!'

'Sure it is.'

'Yes, but it's not real life! You can stay in one spot and live life through your Reppies and do things through your Reppies and if there's danger on the way it overtakes your Reppies, not you. But it's not real life.'

'Amyah—'

'You're not listening! She's not listening!'

'I get it.' Todoma looked her impatience. 'There are limits to what Replicas can do, and what happens to me happens to me.'

'That,' her mother said, 'is not something we should be discussing at your age.'

'She uses them so rarely,' her father murmured. 'Greedy for life, this one.' He took her hand.

'She has eight, actually, not nine.' Had I spoken aloud? I saw Todoma give a warning shake of her head.

'She has what?' exclaimed her mother.

'She has eight replicas, not nine,' I repeated lamely. 'She, um, she lent me one.'

Her parents stared, aghast. Finally her father said, 'You gave a Mhan one of your Replicas? Are you insane?'

Todoma was absorbed in watching her tail.

Her mother looked me up and down. 'What did you do with it? You people don't have Replicas. But you can't get enough of it. I know there's a thriving underground market for it. What did you do—sell it?'

'Amyah!'

'I was just asking. I can ask, can't I? What did you do with it?'

I made myself say it. 'I lost it.'

Her mother stared. 'You lost it?' Slowly she swiveled her head around until she was looking at Todoma. 'He lost it. A Reppie. Your Reppie. These people!'

'Don't call them that!'

'I'll call them whatever I want! They call us cats. We're not cats! E ki le na wayam kami Mhan-nee!'

'I understand Lentishe,' I let her know.

'Then why don't we talk like civilized people?' she snapped. 'Why are we talking common tongue like Mhan peasants?'

I glared at her, then caught myself and looked away. Witch.

Todoma threw up her hands. 'It was just a fafel Replica!'

Her mother looked distraught. 'Are you listening? Did you hear your child?'

'Watch your language, young woman!' said her father.

'They call us cats! Felines. It's in their dictionary!'

'It might be the whiskers,' I told the mother helpfully. 'And the tail.'

She gave me a decidedly evil squint.

Todoma said placatingly, 'I still have eight. I lent him one because—because he misses me when I'm not there. He misses me, Amyah.'

Her father cleared his throat. 'Todoma—'

Todoma looked unhappy, but she also looked stubborn. She looked like she might actually stamp her foot. 'Abah, if you don't like him, say so.'

'I like him. I dare not not like him,' he teased.

'We have been warned.'

Todoma looked from one parent to the other. 'I love him,' she told them quietly. 'He's all I want in the world.'

'We're just worried for you, child.' Her mother's voice was gentle. 'Claws does happen, you know.'

'Not to us,' Todoma said, her tone was fierce and sure. Irrational as it was, I found myself agreeing with her. All of that was the sludge beneath the sea that our intertwined lives floated on, and it was too far away to ever do us harm. Todoma came and stood by me, an arm around my waist. As always there was a stillness and warmth to her that seemed to reek of verdant fields, of dew and honeysuckle, of animals frolicking with their young. My heartbeat quickened as that stillness wrapped itself about me and I saw her again for what she was. We stared at each other without speaking, without smiling. The old cats, watching us solemnly, said nothing at first. And then they made a soft sound, bringing their hands together so the edges touched.

They had given us their blessing.

#

'Doctor? Doctor? Doctor Onyiogwu!'

The past dissolved into Nwa's face.

'Yes?' I put my hands in my pockets.

'Reservations at Shu for the weekend? You said to remind you.'

'Yes, yes, yes. Thank you.'

She nodded and retreated.

I leaned back in my chair and stared at the ceiling.

The wedding had been a quiet affair. Our lives settled into a comfortable rhythm. I would leave the hospital in the evenings and meet her at the university where she taught, the welfare facility where she volunteered, or her worship centre. Todoma was metagnostic and attended the Fellowship of the New Beings, a million-strong assembly headed by a roaring feline behemoth by the name of Prux. I would wait for her outside the building, in the subdued underground street lighting. I would grab and kiss her as soon as she emerged from the open doors, and together we would ascend to the upper levels, into natural light. Days and weeks and months and years sprinted by in this manner, in a happy though occasionally troubled parade, and we sometimes tried to picture what life would have been like if we'd never met, if she hadn't come out to protest a wrong to Mhan, if I hadn't taken a shortcut to work—if, if, if.

In those early years we would wander through the city streets with no destination in mind, liking this in ourselves. Once, strolling through a grounded park, we'd encountered a disturbing but all-too-common spectacle. A very young feline with unformed features was caught in a game of Kickball energetically undertaken by a hooting gang of Mhan teenagers. Instead of rubber or velvet rings they were kicking spiked balls with hard, boot-encased feet. The tiny cat, trembling, would run this way and that, but deadly whooshes of pin-blades blocked his way each time. Whimpering in terror, he kept getting nicked, and he kept falling awkwardly, to the hilarity of the gang. Furious, I jumped in and kicked the ball away, ignoring the sudden pain in my light-shoed foot. Snatching the little one off the ground, a snarl on my face, fear in my heart, I hustled him away from there. He thanked me in a small, breathless voice and scampered off. The teenagers booed me, looking at each other as if to say: Get an eyeful of this stupid ketevel.

I was trembling when I rejoined Todoma.

'It's the way of the world,' she said, noting my fury.

'It's a stupid way.'

'Yes,' she said. She changed the topic. 'Want a pergolat? There's a place nearby.'

'No,' I said. Then, with a sigh: 'Yes.'

We sat at an outdoors eatery and I watched Todoma watch other things. The enormity of existence endlessly fascinated her. A blue star is born, water ripples in a pond, a cloud drifts by, a leaf bends in the wind, a Lentishe walks by, a Mhan stands still, and Todoma's marveling eyes would rise to find the centre of it all. I encountered her returning gaze, and something seemed to run all over me. I grabbed her hand, pressed it convulsively. 'Todoma,' my tone was urgent, 'are you happy with me? Are you happy? I could cut down on work. I could . . .'

She laughed out loud. 'Don't be silly. Don't you be silly now.'

'Doctor!'

Nwa was peering at me from the open doorway. 'Are you all right?' It seemed she had been standing there a while.

'I'm fine, I'm fine. I'm—what is it?'

'You know tomorrow is Eikpo festival.'

'It is?'

She laughed a little. 'How could you forget?'

'Yes, yes. I remember now.' There would, among other things, be a Parade of Masks representing Departed Spirits as well as city and planetary Guardians. There would also be the Iksah pageantry celebrating men and women who had done a great many things for a great many people.

'Can I leave early today?' Nwa asked. 'I'm carrying a Mask and there are rehearsals and...'

'You're carrying a Mask? Nwachakku!' I was

smiling now. 'That's great. Of course you can leave early.'

'Thank you.' She hesitated. 'You'll be there, won't you? Maybe not for my parade but—well . . .' Her eyes began to glow. 'Yaha Misa's being honoured at Iksah this year.'

'She is?'

'He's a he!' Nwa looked scandalised. 'He's a hero! His contributions—wait,' she ordered breathlessly. 'Just wait.' She dashed out and returned moments later, brandishing a book. 'Have you read this? It's called Different and Equal. Listen to this.' She flipped pages and then began to read, her eyes constantly flicking over to me.

'Why push Mhan to do what Lentishe do, as if feline interests are the yardsticks by which all others must stand or fall? Lentishe is not the default specie. Equality is not liking what Lentishe like, or doing what Lentishe do. It's Mhan liking Mhan things and doing Mhan things, and yet being equal just the same . . .'

She closed the book with a snap and looked at me expectantly. I couldn't suppress my smile as I said, 'I'll be there. As much to see Yaha Misa being honoured as to see you carry a Mask. I wouldn't miss it for anything.'

She beamed at me, then spun around and departed in a soft swish of clothing.

I left the office and made my way home. The wind had picked up. The air was fresh and heavy, full of the smell of impending rain. Our home was in a quiet neighbourhood above ground. We had a tree in the front yard, and, here and there, glass fountains spouting out extravagant streams of multi-coloured light. I ran up the steps to the front door and let myself into the house. After I closed the door, Todoma poked her head into the hallway, saw me, and waved. Her head vanished. I found some pergolat on a table and drained it, my tongue snaking around the insides of the cup in quest for more.

Afterwards, I took a shower, and then went into the kitchen to cook while Todoma graded student essays in our study. I took in a tray and we ate there, exchanging news. We could hear thunder and the beginnings of a storm. She strolled over to the window and watched the rain clouds gather. Then she climbed onto the sill and, before I could stop her, shot for the yulo tree outside. My heart leapt into my throat. I was always terrified she would overshoot and miss the branches. I said, 'Are you ever going to stop doing that? A teenager you're not.'

Grinning, she swished her tail briskly back and forth. The wind picked up speed, whipping her hair about her face. She sat, legs swinging, face to the skies. Seconds later the storm broke, letting loose a fury of rain. Todoma whooped and shouted: 'Come on out here! The water's great!'

'You come inside!'

'Come outside! Come on! Come on!' And she laughed in delight. I threw a leg over the windowsill, hesitated, and then retracted it, ignoring Todoma's snicker. I hurried from the room, down the hall, and out the front door. I was drenched by the time I got to the tree. I looked around through a film of water. The streets had cleared, not a soul was in sight. Todoma slid down the tree and took my hand. Her eyes were twinkling.

'Come on!' she cried. We took off together, running through the empty streets. We plunged into any turning that offered itself above ground. We soon found ourselves by a hoverpark. Hand in hand, we made for it. We found a spot we liked and sat. A food vendor pushed his cart past us. He was carrying a rain repeller, and so was quite dry. He gave us a startled glance and offered to share his repeller. We declined with thanks. His own comfort in the face of our exposure to the elements clearly discomfited him. We let him know the water was refreshing. He looked too young and earnest as he told us he was twenty-three and married, one of a Quartet that lived in Ittiwwe Underground, a district two miles north of us. We talked of artificial suns and frozen green lakes and baya vines and other delights of underground living. The boy was enjoyable company. He was recounting an anecdote about the food business, mischief in his eye, when he suddenly started and said, 'What's wrong with your hand?'

That was when Todoma saw it.

I could hear my distressed breathing as I stared at her helplessly. I realised my mouth had fallen open;

I closed it with a snap. My eyes followed hers. The fingers of my right hand were jerking spasmodically, the joints now bending to form a claw, now straightening out. Though it had begun just a few days before, and the episodes were still painless and lasted only seconds, already one thumb wouldn't quite straighten all the way. I looked at the boy but didn't see him anymore, not really, but I heard his voice, low with sympathy, and then he was gone.

Todoma and I stood there and time went away.

At some point I realized that the rain had stopped.

Todoma, who had taken my stricken hand in hers, still hadn't said a word. She seemed to be waiting for something. But I wanted her to speak. I wanted her to say something, anything. I wanted her to—I—I wanted . . .

And suddenly it burst out of me, a tidal outpouring of shame and grief, whose violence took me by surprise. She took me in her arms and I trembled. I'm sorry, I tried to say, but it wouldn't come out right. She shook her head side to side.

'Look,' she said, and pointed. A bhavan had come out of a violet bush, bearing its litter on its back. It looked around anxiously with beady eyes. Seeing us, it waited till it was sure we were no threat, and then began its journey to safer feeding grounds. Sniffling, I watched its progress. It crept over a low wall, its babies dangling on its back and yet firmly in place, and vanished from sight.

'We'll be fine,' Todoma said, but her voice was strange. I remembered, in a flash, other prophecies from long ago. 'I wasn't wrong,' she said to me in that way she had of knowing my thoughts. 'We still have time. Not a lot, but enough.' And she smiled.

I didn't understand, but maybe someday I would. Now, this moment, I was still strong enough to hold her, and we held on as the bhavan's children had. We held on to each other and watched the world, as we always had.

[illegible] ember from fireplace and finished [illegible]
[illegible]

[illegible]
[illegible]
[illegible]
[illegible]
[illegible]

[illegible]
[illegible]
[illegible]
[illegible]

PHOENIX

Famia Nkasa

The day Dalilah left Ghana, clutching the only document that made her human once she got off the plane at the other side, it occurred to her that her student visa could be like a sponge she would scrub herself with. Everything she didn't want to be, she could leave behind in Tamale. Everyone she no longer wanted to love, she could use the gift of distance and time to exorcise.

As the plane climbed farther into the clouds, she did not give any thought to the fact that she was floating up into the kind of cold she would have to learn to wrap around her body like a cloak because fighting it was futile. She was preoccupied with the reinventions she would engineer. What she would mention: the affair she'd had last year with a famous imam's son—it had been tempestuous; the history pamphlet for Senior High School students she'd helped her god-uncle write—she would seem scholarly and important; the fact that she wanted to learn to swing dance—it would add flair to her "differentness" and distinguish her from the lackluster

African students. Then, of course, there were the things she wouldn't speak of unless specifically asked: being a senior prefect at her school—it wasn't cool; being half Christian and half Muslim even though everyone said there was no such thing; the fact that all of her extended family lived outside of Tamale.

Dalilah yearned to rewrite herself simpler and she sensed that this departure might be her chance. She fingered the buckle of her seatbelt as if the solid weight of it (heavy enough to hurt a goat thief if stuffed into a cloth and flung like a slingshot) could keep her from floating out of her skin. She massaged the words that best described her new reality over and over in her mind—"Infinite Possibilities," "Like You'll Never See Me Again," "The Long and Winding Road," "Element of Freedom," "Brand New Me," "The Best is Still Unwritten," until every phrase was supple and fragranced. She wondered if to the other passengers in the plane she was just a girl sitting in Seat 31A, tracing the Pond's-covered pimples on her forehead as she gazed out of the window at the Accra skyline. If so, yawa for dem. She clucked her tongue in pity and smoothed the creases out of her brand-new, powder-blue, trouser suit. They were missing all her truths. She was not basic anymore, oh. She was the personification of the long list of song titles on the back of those pirated CD's sold in traffic.

She rested her chin in her palm and pressed her nose against the glass, wishing she could reach through the window and touch the cottony pallet of clouds. She would be an octopus, extending one languid arm, then another, until she disappeared into them. Reading the safety instruction manual again to keep from bouncing in her seat, she pressed her index finger to the outline of the British Airways logo—so perfectly laminated it was sticky—and traced the letters in a loop. Then she stroked her thumbs over the edges of the page, flattening them out, making them perfect, and smiled at the poetic symmetry in the action.

The chrife girls at school, who thought the only way to be born again was to be washed in the mythical blood of a long-haired, male virgin who went around caressing the festering sores of strangers, had not known what they were talking about. This past year of filling out applications, accepting charity to pay for her SAT's, taking a whole box of Schnapps to her headmaster's house a week before she asked him to write her recommendations, participating in the farce where he acted shocked to be asked and she acted surprised at the suggestion that her earlier gift might have been to sweeten his tongue and loosen his pen, had all been worth it. Forgoing hanging out with her friends every day to go to the Internet café in Education Ridge and use that dial-up service to research subjects for the personal essays most likely to get her admission had all been worth it. Praying and praying every night while she waited to hear back from American universities in tiny cities she'd never heard of, clutching her Muslim tasbih in her right hand and her Catholic rosary in her left and reciting both of them simultaneously (one with her lips and one in her head) all of these choices had yielded fruit. Fruit that was now bursting with nectar and changing the taste of everything it touched for the better. She had her admission letter, her financial aid package, her I-20 admissions certificate, her international student SEVIS number, her passport, her visa, and now her flight. She was off.

She arched into the possibilities of starting over, of choosing who and what to be for the first time in her twenty-year-old life. She savoured the thrilling potential of no longer straddling four worlds. Straddling was a difficult task, whether it be men or worlds. Given a choice between the two, Dalilah would always choose the former, despite the shame it would bring on her family and the damage it would do to her reputation.

Her indulgent grandmother always told her she only thought this because she was still untouched, and had escaped being cut, so the straddling of men's legs held a mystique that she stupidly associated with pleasure. Dalilah always lowered her gaze and pretended to blush—even though, in truth, the imam's son (a hafiz!) had ensured that she was no longer so unsoiled. At least spreading your legs across a man was a natural act, one that resulted in babies. Spreading your self across four identities was not. She hated the daily task of it, the intersections in which you became a Rubik's cube, bending this way and that in different colours and combinations. The mix of diplomacy and impunity required to survive the constant collisions. The adjustment period necessary to go from one place to another without fuelling deep discrepancies between the factions.

So much work. So much grief. First there was World Number One: the upper-class domain of people whose last names were all Mahama, and who she knew only because, years and years before her birth, her grandfather had been their grandfather's garden boy. The Mahamas inhabited a different planet but she was often lumped in with them because she had grown up spending one weekend a month at the Regional Minister's house. Of course, this was only because her mother had continued the tradition of servitude between her family and theirs by being the Minister's personal secretary for as long as anyone could remember.

Dalilah would not call the Minister's children her friends, but they called her theirs. She knew the friendship survived because none of them ever spoke of the fact that on the rare occasions they swung by her house to collect meeting minutes for their father and were forced to drink something, water, at least, they carefully placed the rim of the glass beneath their lower lips so they would not sully the inside of their mouths with whoever's saliva they imagined was still clinging to it. The basket overflowing with delicacies her mother prepared from her most treasured ingredients (things Dalilah and her siblings got to eat only in drawn-out bites at Eid) was always loaded into the boot of their pink Benz with a ceremonious gratitude but promptly given away to the maid or gardener once they got back to their own house on Bolga Road. The friendship survived because Dalilah always made sure to pack her best clothes for the weekends she spent with Abdul, Iddrisu, Salma, and Hamza, and all of them pretended not to notice that her outfits were hand-me-downs or gifts she had gotten from them months before.

Dalilah had learnt as a child that the Mahama's world was best experienced with your eyes closed—if you could pull it off without anyone noticing and smacking you on the shoulder for sleeping while you should be making company with people. The Minister's house was a Dubai hotel. Delicious air-conditioning settled around your shoulders the minute you stepped into the foyer. The hallways were tiled with a granite that chirped beneath your shoes and made you promise yourself you would do the Michael Jackson backslide everywhere instead of ever walking normally again. There was a sitting room, a living room, a parlour room, and a family room (for welcoming different ranks of guests, naturally) and each was a furry, purring cat, with lush carpets, sequined lampshades and relentlessly overstuffed chairs. And the bedrooms? Bosue! The four-poster beds had lace canopies. They cascaded over your skin like rivulets of chilled tiger-nut milk and made you dream gossamer dreams in which you were lighter, happier, and cuter.

Even the kitchen enveloped you with aromas that left you lightheaded. They came from a mixture of smells—smoky peppercorns, syrupy anise, musty cinnamon, pungent dawadawa, throat-tickling capsicum—that ordinary people used in small and solitary increments. Throughout the house, even in the corners of the garage, the thick scent of rich food mingled with the richer smells of French cologne. The olfactory overload had made Dalilah ask her father as a child if even the Mahamas' poopoo was scented. The question, which earned her a knock on the head, was never answered.

Now she was going to America. She would never be knocked again. She would buy her own clothes, create the smells she wanted in her very own house. She would never have to bite her tongue until it bled because everyone else had such a fondness for the unspoken. She nodded at the impending fulfilment of her promise to herself and pressed that wonderful little button on her armrest till her chair became a lounger. Aaaaaaaaaaaaaaaaaaah. Nice! She lifted the armrest between her seat and the empty middle seat. Then lifted the armrest between the middle seat and the empty aisle seat, impressed by the little sofa she was creating. She stretched her legs out and laid her jacket on her lap. A wheeze of delight escaped her lips as she settled back onto the three plane-issued pillows that came with the seats. She snuck her hands under her jacket and locked and unlocked her seatbelt to the rhythm of the ditty she was humming under her breath.

That was a first for her. You see, whether it was sitting stiffly in a private car with the Mahamas, taking a loori with friends from school, gripping the waist of a stranger astride one of the okadas that ferried everyone everywhere in Tamale, or even just walking down the street, she was a complete stranger to the sweetness of solitude. There was no such thing in any of her worlds. Not in World Number One, where the Minister's minions buzzed around, fixing this and straightening that, and his oversized family was constantly engaging with her to prove to themselves what enlightened people they were.

Particularly not in World Number Two: the solidly working-to-middle class neighbourhood where her parents' government-owned cottage nestled among those of all the other employees of Tamale's ministries and NGO's. The overcrowded hamlet was a five-mile radius of glorified civil servants basking in the prestige of their affiliations and camouflaging the indignity of their positions. From Baba Nukuru, who walked with his slender nose in the air as if he thought that that would distract everyone from the fact that his big toe had liberated itself from the front of the work shoes he refused to toss because they had been imported from Italy instead of made in a factory in Kumasi—to Hajia Saafiyah, whose children smelt like rancid wagashi but slurred all their words in a locally acquired foreign accent—this world was an Africa Magic movie filled with Nollywood characters.

Dalilah's mother often told her to be proud that she stayed on Zongo Street and to make sure that every time she got in a loori, and told the driver's mate where she was going, she remembered to mention that she lived there, emphatically enough for all the people bathing in each other's sweat on the peeling seats of public transport to hear. Whenever Umi got on this soapbox, Dalilah rolled her eyes till she could feel them scraping the top of her skull. Yet, since she was a child, she had developed the habit of stepping with the ball of her left foot into the entrance of the Zutong minibus, hunching her right shoulder past the sliding door so she could sidle in without snagging her clothes on protruding bits of metal, and then, with her other foot still in midair, saying, "Please, I am going HOME to Zongo Street," before handing over her loori fare to the mate.

And yes, sometimes some elderly Nanumba woman on the bus would primp down the lacy insets of her djellaba, adjust her headscarf till it fell over the tribal marks on her bleached cheeks, turn to Dalilah with an excitedly enquiring "Hmmmmm?" and pat the seat next to her with a toothy smile. For the rest of the ride, Dalilah would be cuddled by this matronly stranger and asked if it was true that the houses on Zongo Street had been built by Kwame Nkrumah himself after Independence, and he himself had lived in one for a few weeks while he was overseeing the formation of the ministries in the Northern Region. She would be asked if it was true that noooooobody in a house on Zongo Street shared a courtyard or went to Alhajia Abudu's place to watch television or listen to radio because every family had one of those machines to themselves. Was it true that everyone who lived there used a room inside the house to do their business and sat, instead of squatted, every time they emptied their stomachs—on a white throne made of ivory no less?

Dalilah would nod yes and explain how their water closet worked (on the days the taps were running). The woman would clap her hands together with glee, releasing koose-redolent traces of the breakfast still languishing under her nails into the air till half the bus was muffling sneezes, and exclaim that "The houses must have been originally intended for white people and Southerners, they sounded so nice!" Then Dalilah's new friend-by-force would invariably mention a son, nephew, or grandchild who was a naturally bright boy, it had been obvious since the first time he came up with that more ingenious way to lock the cattle in the kraal, and he was now in Tamale Secondary School, and the oasis of her Sahel and Insha'Allah in the name of the Prophet Mohammed Sallallahu Alayhi Wasallam he would get good marks and go to Training College and maybe one day live in one of those nice houses on Zongo Street where she could come and visit him. Dalilah would bite the inside of her cheek to maintain a straight face, try not to focus on the eerie resemblance the remaining kola-nut stained teeth inside the woman's mouth bore to the outside walls of the Larabanga mosque, nod reverently, and say " Ii M'ma, inshallah, it will come to pass." Then when the loori passed the Ahmadiya Mosque, sped by Zogbeli, Lamakara and Lamashegu, wobbled behind Sakasaka, wound around the Kalpuhin Estates and reached Zongo Street, she would point out the pink and green three-bedroom cottage where she lived with her mother, four brothers, three sisters, and two cousins. Her awed admirer would crane her neck to take in every detail of the walls and the gate. Then, she would press the banana leaf of tsire-suya or balango she had intended for her own lunch into Dalilah's hand before the young lady nudged past the knees of the other passengers and disembarked.

On the days that this happened, Dalilah would be sure to wait until she got home to open the treat so she could share it with the clamouring horde of siblings. She would answer the question of where she got the street food from with a dramatic re-enactment of her loori adventure—exaggerating the details for her mother's benefit because she knew it would make her happy. It would take the poor woman's mind off the fact that school fees were due for the youngest two, and she had promised Ibrahim a new uniform in time for the field trip to Mole Park but everyone knew salaries were going to be a few weeks late because the Minister had travelled again. It would make the poor woman forget the shame she felt when they visited her husband's family in the village and she saw with her own two eyes that her children often ate better there than they did at home. Dalilah would play up the recent interaction, mimicking the Nanumba lady to thigh-slapping laughter from her audience. She would always offer her mum the last morsel of the treat their prestigious neighborhood had brought them and wait until the proud woman turned her nose up at it, declaring she had no idea which squalid alley of debauchery the geriatric had purchased it from, before popping it contentedly into her own mouth.

The contentment always evaporated though once the last flavours receded from Dalilah's tongue. At that point, she would slink away from the chaos into the bedroom she shared with the rest of the girls, climb on the bottom bunk and turn her back to the door. She would pull single hairs out of her eyebrows with her fingers, relishing the stings of pain, idly arranging the follicles into stick figures on a sheet of white paper and shaking her head with gratitude that Rafiatu or any of the others from World Number Three weren't currently visiting and did not have to witness everyone giggling at "squalid alley of debauchery" and arguing about which TV character Umi had learnt the phrase from. She wouldn't have been able to look at her cousins. How? It was from some such squalid alley of debauchery that all of the food they ate was from.

It was from some such squalid alley of debauchery that all the food she herself devoured, whenever she spent holidays with them deep in the Gumbihini slums, was purchased. And when her mother was there, visiting with her older brothers and their wives, perched on a broken stool in the courtyard they shared with ten other families, she shut up and ate whatever she was offered. There was no trace of that woman in the dusty sitting room, preening like a peacock as she spoke English that was too big for her mouth. Not in Gumbihini, where sewage mixed with food cooking on open fires mixed with sweat and the cheapest of cheap cosmetics like a metaphor for life: our waste, our nourishment, our effort, our effort to cover up our effort. Not in that place that exhilarated and unsettled strangers until they became confused about what the true shape of life was. Not in that place that even smelled like chaos and forced you to breathe through your mouth because inhaling made you hungry and nauseous at the same time.

"Which version of herself would her mother be if she was with her on this flight right now?" Dalilah wondered. "Hm?" "Which one?" This plane smelled nothing like chaos. It was fresh like the inside of a straight-from-the-factory fridge. It smelt of new money, still cold from the vault, untouched by any transaction and impervious to the influence of the outside environment. And now, actually, also like some indecipherable... herbal... tropical... overpowering...? Eucalyptus? Lotion? Shampoo?

Dalilah opened her eyes. An air hostesses' hair was brushing her shoulder as the woman tapped her arm. It took all Dalilah's sangfroid to not visibly startle and she enjoyed a frisson of pride when she managed to look up calmly with an inviting smile. She did not get one in return. The British Airways pin on the starched blue jacket seemed to be winking at her but the woman's mouth was a slit in the square of her face. As she spoke, her tone held that coldness of market women when a customer has haggled down to a price that will disrupt their projected earnings for that day.

Dalilah nodded mutely at the curt instruction to put her seat back into the upright position until they had been airborne for a sufficient amount of time. She deactivated the recline feature and sat up straight. The lady gestured impatiently to the raised armrests of the other seats. Dalilah put those down too, bereft as her nice sofa turned once more into three small cages. She flushed, then flushed at herself for flushing, for feeling scolded by such an impersonal reprimand, particularly one from a shapeless woman with dry yellow hair that smelt like fruit salad stored in a medicine cabinet. Feeling gye when she was nothing more than a waitress in the sky. Mtscheeew. Dalilah tapped her burning cheeks to cool them. Her eyes bored a hole into the woman's back as she continued down the aisle giving select passengers curt instructions.

After glancing around to see if anyone had noticed her comeuppance, she grabbed her jacket and shoved her arms into it as if the extra layer of clothing would offer some kind of protection. She smoothed down first one lapel, then another, then both at the same time. Watching her fingers perform each soft efficient motion, as if she were wiping the interaction with the air hostess off her chest, brought back her mellow contentedness. She pressed the side of her arms against her breasts and smiled down at them, enjoying their pear-shaped firmness under her shirt. Yakubu, the first boy who had ever touched them, would currently be on the loori heading back to Gumbihini from his stall at the market. Even though she had dumped him years ago, he had given her a small bottle of scented powder when she told him she was leaving. She had rubbed some under her arms the last time she saw him and as she waved and waved at his dwindling figure from her mother's old Peugeot she had put her nose to her armpit and inhaled his gift, feeling as if she was taking some of Gumbihini back home to Zongo Street with her. Now it felt like she was taking some of Gumbihini to America with her. Would she feel that way every time she squeezed her breasts? Could Yakubu see her plane from below? Were all the little kids in Gumbihini looking up at it now and were they elbowing each other out of the way and waving at the white line in the sky?

Dalilah chuckled at how ironic it was, that, after all the efforts her parents had made to ingratiate her into World Number One and give her a sense of hauteur about World Number Two, World Number Three was the one she would miss the most. It was filled with the people she loved the deepest, the ones she felt were most unfettered by life's rules, the ones she judged as being most truly themselves. So many of the true things she knew about life she had learned in those slums.

One Saturday she had been forced to run more than three kilometres at full speed to get help because Minister Mahama's son, Abdul, who had insisted on following her to Gumbihini, had gotten on the bad side of some Gurunsi kids with his ethnic slurs about their heritage. They had thrown him into a gutter full of unmentionables. Abdul had flailed like he was drowning, even though the algae-thickened water only came up to his ribs. He had tried to claw his way out yet kept sliding on Pure Wata wrappers and moss-green scum, slipping back down into the floating piles of cow dung, horse shit, and human waste, as the Gurunsi boys pointed, whooped, and humped the air. Maaata! The frogs and tadpoles in the gutter had started swimming to the surface and were leaping up his shirt.

Poor overfed Abdul had been too shocked to do anything but sputter, squeak, and wail and after trying to clamber out the fifth or sixth time he had given up, just stood there in the gutter, put his hands on his head and started to cry. He had never been treated that way. Everyone he knew knew that he was the Minister's son. In a place like the Northern Region—removed as it was, part of a country that deigned to claim it only from afar—the Minister was the President's representative here on earth like the Pope was God's—and Abdul, as his son, was like the representative's representative.

Dalilah had been aware that no one had ever had the gumption to tell the pudgy dimwit that in some places people were so removed from power that it meant something different to them. People were so focused on survival that their children had little time to participate in adult affairs. They had no need to know who was in charge of what. Not beyond their immediate needs. Knowing Alhaji Rafiq had the keys to the public toilet? That was knowledge with use. Being able to recognize the Minister himself, much less one of his however-many sons, had absolutely no value. In these playgrounds, respect was demanded with immediacy because actual currency was scarce. Calling Gurunsi boys names when you didn't know how to fight and couldn't beat them was stupid. She had considered being the first to impart this advice to Abdul but she knew it would be unwelcome and would only make things bad for her mother if she did. So there had been little to do but run for help.

Abdul had been unceremoniously fished out

by her uncle Khalil, hosed off, and sent home in his chauffeur-driven Range Rover. When Dalilah got back to Zongo Street she had gotten such a dressing-down she felt the words searing her skin. A week or two afterwards, her mother had come home and said, with a see-what-you-have-wrought toss of her hands, that there had been a cabinet meeting in anticipation of a visit from the President, and the Minister had pontificated for hours about razing the slums in Gumbihini to show how progress was being made in the region's social development projects. Dalilah had run to the bathroom and thrown up all over the floor even though there was no running water to clean the vomit up. Luckily nothing came of it. The President cancelled his visit to focus on some problems in the Ashanti and Central regions and life went on.

Dalilah could not. The thought that through whatever the world decided to throw at her—in spite of whatever circumstance caused the arbiter of her fate to change from herself to some untouchable entity—she was supposed to rebound and plod on, made sense in her head but not in her heart. Something started to make her itch. All the time. Scratching did no good. It felt as if the itch was in the marrow of her bones. On her next visit to World Number Four, the village in the Upper East Region where the bulk of her relatives lived, she found herself sobbing on her grandmother's shoulder.

There had been a total lack of preamble. M'ma Meimuna had exclaimed, "Oy Dalilah. Nyini n bala? " when she heard footsteps at the hearth, the warmth of her voice streaming through her hut into the open air. Dalilah responded that, yes, it was indeed her at the door, and teasingly asked M'ma Meimuna what sorcery she had obtained as a newlywed that enabled her to accurately guess the visitor from the sound of their footsteps. M'ma Meimuna ran out to welcome her granddaughter, clasping Dalilah's face, pinching her cheeks, and saying that, ah, what kind of stupid question was that, she had tended to her since she was born, she could pick her voice out of a choir on the radio, the sound of her breath out of a windstorm. By the time the old lady's pillowy arms encircled Dalilah her floodgates had burst open.

She cried with her whole body. The phlegm running down her chin, the manic heaving of her chest and the gyrations of her shoulders had given the sobs a theatrical intensity as they echoed against the rounded clay walls. M'ma Meimuna squeezed her tightly, asking what the matter was, exclaiming that among her forty-five grandchildren there were definitely a few random criers but Dalilah had never been one of them, so she was making her very scared. Was someone dead? Had one of her son's or daughter's in Tamale been maimed? She gripped Dalilah and bent her backwards to study her face. Had she been defiled? Dalilah giggled between tears and said no, no, no, nothing was wrong, no one was dead and that she herself was just as shocked at this outburst of tears.

She pushed back into the old lady's embrace. She glanced through the window of the hut, past the compound, to the surrounding landscape. This place, Nakudungu, felt as familiar to her as the shapes of her teeth. It was flat. Sparse. Visiting it was strolling inside an open wound. When you walked to the edge of the village and looked across the earth, you felt like you yourself were vast and endless, and Dalilah managed to convince herself and her grandmother that it was the dryness encroaching from the north, eating the bush so fast that every few months Nakudungu looked bigger and starker than when you had last seen it, the shock of that, was what had made her cry. The savannah turning into the Sahel and the Sahel turning into the Sahara, and their village being obliterated by the desert like it had never even existed, that was something to cry about. Wasn't it? M'ma Meimuna exhaled, squishing Dalilah into her bosom and telling her she was a good girl, a pious girl, for caring so much about the ancestral land.

The compliment, though unearned, was not untrue. World Number Four, this village where her ancestors had settled, where her blood was from, was the place where Dalilah had learned to peel yam with such precision that no more than a centimeter of white came off with the brown outer skin. It was the place where her grandaunts had taught her how to select the sweetest tiger-nuts and how to make ataadwe milk from scratch. It was the place where everyone, even elders, treated her as if a halo shone on her because she came from Tamale, even though, ironically, on the few occasions she had gone to Accra, everyone there had treated her as if she was a kayayoo covered in mud because she came from Tamale.

True, Nakudungu was also the place where, from the minute you got off the loori, a film of red dust covered your feet, ankles and shins till it was almost at your knees (the Southerners at school called it Sahara stockings), and because of that it was the one place she visited where she never took pictures unless she could make sure the lens only caught the top half of her body. Yes, it was also the place where everything she did was haram and the cause of fitnah, while nothing her brothers did ever came under any scrutiny. It was the place where poorer relatives misled you about the prices of things and you were never sure who truly loved you and wanted you to prosper and who would steal hair out of your comb to take to the Mallam so he could conjure up a jinn to plant inside your body. It was the place where there was always the risk of committing a faux pas because there were so many people to remember and you could never be up to date on who and who were fighting and who and who were currently in what sub-clique of the family. But M'ma Meimuna already knew that so there was no need to say it.

And besides, wasn't that the nature of all the four worlds she was from? Wasn't that the nature of all this straddling, all this bifurcating, in her case "quadfurcating"? The worlds she loved were the ones she would rather commit suicide than inhabit permanently. The ones she could live in, she loathed. Chale. The universe itself was complicated enough. Loving things you could not be proud of made little bits of bone grind up against each other inside your chest and eventually your heart would wear itself thin and give in. Four worlds? That was three too many. Then you factored in the other worlds within the four? The posses? The factions? Tsk tsk tsk tsk. They were responsible for all six of her prematurely grey hairs and she was sure they would turn her whole head white someday soon.

On this plane there were no factions, only… choices. Handbag in the overhead bin or under the seat in front of you? "Wine or spirits?" "Coca-Cola or orange juice?" "Ice or no ice?" "Chicken or beef?" Even the orderly little rectangles of personal amenities all to oneself —a reading light, a fan, an earphone outlet— meant that what happened to the general population of the plane was something one only had to put up with if one wanted to. Just because the plane chose to sleep didn't mean that you had to. Just because everyone was watching a movie didn't mean you couldn't decide to listen to music instead. Even in the vessel that was ferrying you to a new land, God was trying to make it clear that you were entering a world of individual destinies.

On this plane, bright and sanitized, carpeted everywhere (even on the walls) there were no allegiances. There was only air. Air so rarefied all of them inhaling it were unified by the minty mist snaking into their nostrils. This air was so cold it was visible to the human eye; it changed shapes like a choir of necromancers as it slithered out of the honeycomb vents between the overhead baggage and the buttons above the plane seats. This air was so powerful it could cool you from the inside out, it could waft right through your chest and reconfigure the internal structure of your heart until only the most important spaces for the most important people were left. It could become a surgeon performing a bypass or a contractor refurbishing a dilapidated building. This air was so clean it could blow away any past, any dust, any particles clinging to the pores of your skin.

Dalilah did not know much but she knew enough to know that coming from where she was coming from, and going to where she was going to, she would already be odd enough—already be weighty and difficult to digest in this soft-stomached world of blue-veined people. Without writing herself simpler, without subjugating some nuance so that a clear narrative could be established, she would never survive the possible depths of misunderstanding. She had been told once, by her cousin by marriage four times removed on her mother's side—a bright-skinned, handsome boy who had gotten a scholarship to study in

London and had come back home to a cushy job and a big house in Takoradi—that it was possible to buff her history so smooth that hairline fissures just thin enough to slot her dreams into would appear. She wanted that so badly.

Yet, inexplicably, a part of her also wanted nothing more than for the plane to develop engine trouble when it stopped in Kano and be forced to land. From Kano she could jump on a bus. She would be home in a day.

And when, of course, it didn't, delaying for only an hour as it boarded its Nigerian contingent before it lifted off to the pilot's voice over the public address system making sure all the new passengers were comfortable and secured—for the first time since she had decided that come hell or high water she would go to America, Dalilah felt that thing, the thing that made Lot's wife steal the last glance, tugging her throat through her stomach. She squeezed her eyes shut and turned away from the window. All that she had known would soon become a porridge of streets and neighbourhoods. Then it would morph into a marriage of tiny lights. Then it would shrink to a dim glow and finally to nothing. Suddenly the world beneath her became something she would willingly turn to salt to be able to turn back and look at one final time.

"The sky will have to be your sire from now on," proclaimed a pudgy, French-sounding man as he plopped down in the empty seat next to her. He proclaimed his edict with an affected flourish. He had been on the other side of the aisle in seat 31 E, trapped between a Ethiopian trader reading a guidebook of Chinese conversations and a white girl with long dreadlocks who looked like she showered with dirty oil.

Like every other passenger on the plane, he had just been a peripheral character in the stage play the universe was writing about her new life, so dealing with him up close, and so unexpectedly, hardened Dalilah's jaw. He plunked down his overnight bag in the empty seat to the right of him, casually used her lap as a holding place for his laptop, slipped off his loafers, tucked them under the seat and then retrieved his machine from her lap without any apology for the fact that his hand had brushed against the mound of her crotch. Pinpricks tingled up Dalilah's spine and teased the tips of her ears. Her hand instinctively balled into a fist. The French-sounding man tucked his overnight bag under the seat it had been on, wiggled his toes inside their plaid socks, and then reclined his chair without buckling his seatbelt, as if to prove he could deliberately flaunt airline instructions. Dalilah looked around for the too-knowing chick who had chastised her but she was back by the toilets. The other air hostesses, marching up and down the aisle like schoolchildren on Independence Day, said nothing.

Dalilah signalled to one of them. She seemed to be in charge. She wanted this older lady with waxy lipstick to ask the French-sounding man some important questions—"Why was his seat reclined and his seatbelt unbuckled even though they had just taken off again?" "Why had he migrated to her row instead of remaining in his assigned seat?" "More importantly, if he had seen the seats next to her still unfilled after leaving Kano and thought he should share in her bounty, why was he sitting right next to her when he could have sat in the aisle seat and left a space between them?" "Did he think the aeroplane was for his uncle?" Dalilah wanted the air hostess to hold him by the scruff of the neck and not let him go till he provided satisfactory responses. Then she wanted the woman to thwack him over the head with a duty-free catalogue and send him back to the seat he came from.

Yet when the air hostess leaned over him to ask Dalilah, "Yes, love?" with a mix of indulgence and irritation, all the words she wanted to say came to mind in Dagbanli. She opened her mouth to state her case. The first non-English syllable started to tumble out. She shook her head in horror and raised a quivery hand in a gesture of dismissal instead. The air hostess waited for a few seconds to see if Dalilah would recover and remember what she wanted, then shared a long-suffering sigh with the French-sounding man and swivelled away.

The triumphant Frenchman beamed at Dalilah and chucked her under the chin. He muttered something. All Dalilah's words were still in her mother tongue so she just blinked. Repeatedly. The Frenchman seemed to think the source of her shock and confusion was whatever gibberish he had said when he first sat down. He repeated it "The sky will have to be your sire." He even added the same absurd gesture from before as if he was drawing a backwards letter "C" or about to curtsy to a king.

Dalilah's face unfroze. Her left eyebrow shot up. "It means your father" he clarified, as if the only baffling thing about what had just happened was the antiquated English word he had used. Dalilah scratched at a pimple on her chin, popping it surreptitiously between her thumb and index finger and swiping her hanky over the pus before it oozed down her skin. She shifted in her seat until she was melding her body to the wall. She didn't think she could bear to look out of the window until they reached an altitude where everything faded to black and her nostalgia firmly retreated to its proper place behind her excitement. But she also could not bear to look at the Frenchman. So she just stared at the back of the seat in front of her. "The sky would have to be her sire?" What kind of nyaa was that?

The Frenchman nudged her. "The clouds will be your family," he said. "America, well, America will be your benevolent parent." He seemed to think he was in a poetry recital. He had even introduced two new hand flourishes. Dalilah was not sure what to feel. Bombarded? Defeated? Those were the obvious choices but it seemed unfair to allow a stranger the intimacy of that kind of effect on her. She was even less certain of how to respond. But, Subn'allah, she had not been raised to ignore adults who were talking to her. Years of socialization asserted themselves, winding themselves parasitically around her anger and sucking the vim out of it, and she nodded as politely as she could manage and choked out an "I see," then batted tears of frustration that her traitorous English had returned in this time of less-greater need.

She dug her nails into her thigh at the realization that the Frenchman assumed she was leaving for school, or for life, as opposed to a holiday or even just for the weekend. She was miffed he could presume, despite her suit and new Nike slip-on sneakers, which she had scrubbed every bit of dirt from with a toothbrush, that she didn't come from a life that one wouldn't want to escape, a life that just had to be offering far less than whatever was waiting for her on the other side. It undid her that he guessed from her attire, or from her demeanor, or from the way she spoke English—crisper than anyone she knew apart from the Mahama children but still short somehow.

She wanted to ask him how he knew, when even the Immigration Agent at the U.S. Embassy had, when she said she was going to study in America so she could come back and start an NGO to help her people in the North, nodded approvingly and then granted her visa with a smile. But she was aware that the Frenchman's response, whatever it was, would hurt her. So she just gave him a stiff smile and wrote a script in her head in which she was sucking her teeth at this runny-faced toke with eyes the colour of week-old waakye, cursing him, his mother, and his eternal descendants, wrapping a lapa around her hips and tying it into a knot to let him know she was ready to fight, and then pummelling him with her fists and her saliva. What was it about her leaving home, on a full scholarship to Bryant & Stratton College in Wisconsin no less, that made him assume that her family was no longer capable of caring for her, that her father would stop fathering her, that her mother would die, that she had been transformed into some orphan?

She fished in her seat pocket for her MP3 player and stuck its earphones in her ears. Perhaps it was this no-name, third-rate contraption which M'ma Meimuna had sold all her guinea fowls to buy that gave her away as some kind of Johnny-Just-Come. Or, more precisely, some Johnny-first-time-going-planning-to-overstay-the-student-visa-and-work-some-job-where-you-earn-wages-not-salary-till-she-married-a-citizen-and-got-her-papers. She wished she had a fancy iPod with which to ignore this Frenchman and she felt a surge of anger at herself for being so grateful for her grandmother's gift, so misty already for her love—so touched by the pride with which M'ma Meimuna had opened the packet and showed Dalilah how the earphones went inside the small hole in the machine and the tears in her yellowing eyes as she had said "Go well, light of my heart"—that she had packed this Made in China trash with a complete lack of hesitation. The earphones weren't even working properly. The Azonto beat of her favorite E.L. song was just a whisper. She hoped her neighbour couldn't tell and would take the hint that she was unavailable for further conversation. Alas, it was not to be so.

"You need to take care of your passport," the Frenchman said, gesturing at the small green book that had tumbled from her armrest into his seat. Dalilah grabbed at it before he could pick it up and hand it to her. She hated the way he said "passport", as if it was two words rather than two syllables. He pronounced it "passed port," like he thought it was some missed opportunity. "Passed port." As if they were travelling by ship and the document in her hand was a series of docks they had failed to stop at, some infinite possibility they had ignored and would live to regret.

She hated his accent. His stupid face like a monkey's shadow. The way he refused to move despite her eloquent body language. The way he leaned into her space to pluck her passport from her hand, gripped tightly in her fist though it was—flipping through its pages and examining her visa and telling her she shouldn't have any trouble when she got to America, they would probably permit her to enter the country, the stamp looked real enough, and her country wasn't known for its crooks like Nigeria or its jihadist refugees like Somalia, so as long as she emphasized what kind of African she was, and looked the immigration officer in the eye, she should be okay. Though it was a shame Ghana had converted to the ECOWAS passport—The Third World just liked to copy blindly, non? The Economic Community of West African States was not the European Union, for goodness sake, so why this one-passport thing, anyway? It was a mistake, Mon Dieu, it was such a mistake, because the fact that the Ghana passport was blue (like the American one, non?) that had been a plus, a big plus, a real plus. Now, they had changed it to the same ugly colour as the Nigerian passport, which as far as he was concerned the border officials of the world were well within their rights to have a visceral aversion to, considering the 491'ers or 941'ers, or whatever they were called, who kept sneaking into civilized countries to commit fraud and do crimes, aiee, Ghana had just made things harder for their citizens, and actually "Quel dommage, mon petit chou," now that he considered all the factors, with her "Islamic" name she may not have it so easy.

This Frenchman. The audacity of an ant. Dalilah was furious at his insolence, at his impression that she needed his help in some way, at his insouciant insistence that his unsolicited opinion would be not only welcome but adhered to. She was even more peeved to be grateful for the information.

As an African living in the world, a Northerner living in Ghana, a woman living in Tamale, having no alternative but to accept help from entities she despised and who she was certain had nothing but the most patronizing and supercilious disregard for her was a familiar sentiment. But it did not make the humiliation any easier or the violence coursing through her body any less potent. She had not known that the thing in her passport, with her picture, the watermarked U.S.A coat of arms, all those official-looking SEVIS numbers and miscellaneous bells and whistles, that holy grail called an F-1 visa, was just a very expensive permission slip to get on the plane, be flown to an American airport, walk up to the Homeland Security employee behind the counter and make a humble request to be allowed in. She had not known that it did not guarantee her entry into the U.S.

She'd been unaware that it was like a flier to a party, but one at which there was a bouncer at the door—and her dress, her appropriateness, her ability to assure him that she was simply coming to the party and leaving, not planning to grind inappropriately against any boys, start any fights, drink any free liquor that had not been supplied for the likes of her, and, of course, leave when she was asked to, was what would dictate the actual permission to attend the party. But now she knew. She was glad she knew. Though she still hated the Frenchman.

Only now, she hated even more, this nameless, faceless, bouncer of an immigration officer she would meet when she landed.

She practiced saying her name and smiling. She rehearsed how she would hand the border agent her passport. She examined the nails on each of her hands before deciding on her left, because none of the polish on those fingers was chipped and it would make a better impression when she slid it across the counter. She planned the major she would mention. On her I-20 they had listed her major as "undecided." She hadn't arrived at Bryant & Stratton yet so how could she know what she was studying? For American universities, a major was not supposed to be necessary at this phase of things. But after this series of revelations, she didn't need the Frenchman to tell her that "I don't know yet" or "I am still deciding" would be good enough for someone coming from a country that smelled more like America but probably not for her.

She needed a major. She thought about saying Electrical Engineering, but, then, maybe the immigration officer might think she was coming to learn how to make bombs. She fiddled with Chemistry, then she remembered Abdulmutallab, that rich Nigerian boy the Mahamas were related to on their Hausa side, who had smuggled the weapons of mass destruction in his underpants and been on a flight going to Detroit from Ghana when his liquid bomb caught fire. He had been a Chem student. Uh-

uh. That wouldn't do. Hm. Physics? No. Too linked to that stuff. She settled on Biology. That was the major she would mention. Human biology, she would specify, so the INS agent didn't think she was interested in biological terrorism. Human Biology. Doctors were welcome everywhere.

She pulled out the small mirror from her bag and checked if her face-powder had faded, turned on her in-flight screen to see how far they had gotten from Kano—they were over Yaoundé now—and then peeked out of the corner of her eye at what lay outside her window. Thankfully, it seemed to be all black. It was safe to look again. The Frenchman was nattering on about how racism was strong in America but because of their guilt about the past they liked Africans better than their own black people so she should be sure to not become too "yo-yo-bling-bling-Jay-Z" or she might be mistaken for one of them and, unlike France, which was the most equal place in the world because French people they didn't see color (Liberte, Egalite, Fraternite was what their country was built on, did she know that?) America was built on killing the Indians and eating Big Macs and collecting money and even the money they didn't really have anymore... but Dalilah completely tuned him out, home training be damned. She presented him with her back and pressed her nose to the window till her breath made circles on the glass.

With nothing but the night sky to compete with, the endless white road of the aeroplane's wing looked like a fashion runway; the kind you could strut down in a fabulous outfit before stepping off into the endless opportunity of the galaxy. How would she walk up to the immigration officer's station? Like a model? Shoulders back, stomach in, head straight? Hips swaying? Full sashay? Smile fixed? Yes. That was it. She would greet him with her poshest "Hello." Ask how he was doing with a charming lilt. Then say, "I'm here to begin my matriculation at Bryant & Stratton College, please. Here are my documents." She practiced under her breath until she was satisfied she could execute the phrase flawlessly. Then she proceeded to map out her new life, envisioning scenario after scenario of awesomeness, until she was once again a frothing ocean of possibility. She walked three fingers back and forth across the left side of her chest, tracing an outline for the tattoo she'd get as soon as she'd saved up the money. It would be a phoenix—in red, gold, and green, with two black stars for eyes, flying upwards towards her collarbone with its wings outstretched. There'd be a ribbon in its beak with the word "SOAR" written on it in some undulating script.

THE DO-GOODERS

Lauri Kubuitsile

I suppose I knew all along that we were poor. I put it down to the nonsense of the adults more than anything else. But I blame the do-gooders on my sister who made us a target for them in the first place. They'd been scouting us ever since we lived in the cottage on the lake with a hundred cats and René decided she wanted to go to church.

We weren't church people. At least not the churches of the Protestants with their tame white walls and bloodless Jesus. If we went to church at all, it was to the Catholic Church, where the sun shone through the gory pictures of suffering in the windows and, at the front, watching over it all, was the real Jesus, with sharp thorns poking into his head and blood dripping into his sorrow-filled eyes. The Catholic Church was about suffering. René's church was all about finding someone to help, whether they wanted it or not.

It all started that summer on the lake. When I look back I suppose I shouldn't blame René. She was fifteen years old, and, being fifteen, she was busy looking for a boyfriend and decided that Jimmy Reynolds, the Protestant minister's son, would be a good target. So Jimmy Reynolds came out to the lake and rowed about in the boat my mother stole from next door. Jimmy didn't see the situation clearly, at least not right away. Living on the lake with a boat and a hundred cats looks even a bit posh to an untrained eye. Besides, he was still distracted by René's newly grown breasts that filled out the cups of the red bikini she'd bought at K-Mart.

My mother wasn't happy about the whole thing. 'I don't trust a boy who's so clean,' she told René, her green eyes squeezed up into mean-guy slits. My mother was used to my brother Mike, who didn't bathe during school holidays, unless swimming counted, and everyone knew it didn't. 'Besides,' she said, blowing perfect smoke rings out of her fire engine-red lipstick-covered lips, 'You must watch out for those Protestants. They just take life too easy. Way too easy.'

René spouted back. 'I'll do what I want. Anyways, there's nothing you can do, I've already joined their church.'

A quiet hush filled the one-room cement cottage while we waited for my mother to blow. The only noise was the whine of Felix, giving birth to her third litter of kittens born that summer. My mother kept silent, always something to fear, and René slammed out the screen door. The summer progressed with my mother's unresolved silence lingering in the humid air.

At that point in our lives, me and René and Mike were living with my mother and had been for about two years. My father was somewhere we didn't quite know, but when my mother had a few too many 'black days' he'd come back and pack us up and take us away to his place. His place changed a lot depending on his latest girlfriend. Last time his place was Barbara's place. She was okay if you like tight pink dresses, curlers and red nails. I didn't. René loved Barbara, who taught her how to pluck her eyebrows into surprised curves and to paint her toenails without getting nail polish on her skin. When we left, René cried for a whole week.

We moved to the cottage by the lake when school closed in June. We moved for the same reason we always did: my mother didn't pay the rent and we were evicted. The law was that you could only be evicted if you failed to pay rent for three months, so normally we stayed in a place just over three months when we lived with my mother. In a way, I liked it. I didn't waste time making friends and trying to fit in anywhere because I knew that we'd be leaving. René was always tearing bits of her heart off and leaving them behind. Her crying christened every new house.

We sailed through the summer. My mother ignored René's comings and goings; she was too busy with the cats anyway. We found most of them there. The cottage had been abandoned for many years and the cats had taken up residence. Others might have chased them off but my mother, a victim of one too many evictions herself, refused. Mike and I loved it. We'd never had pets before. Though most of the cats were too wild to catch, the baby kittens could be trapped in a corner and grabbed up. They hissed and spat and clawed us up and down our arms, but eventually if we held them enough they'd calm down. By the end of summer some were even purring next to our heads on the pillow when we fell asleep at night.

One evening, as the sun was sinking under the edge of the lake and we were sitting out on the rickety pier, a car pulled up. A tall man in ironed shorts and a collared golf shirt and his tiny wife, who was dressed in a pastel sweater set, got out and came walking towards us. They stopped at the edge of the pier and the man spoke. 'Can I ask what you're doing here?'

My mother looked up from the kittens on her lap. 'Why, of course you can, it's a free country, or so I've heard.' She went back to petting the cats.

The man looked at his wife who clung a bit tighter on his muscled arm. 'This is private property. It belongs to the Millers down in Chicago and I believe that boat you've got tied to the pier is ours.'

'Well, is it now? You shouldn't leave your boat floating in the water untied, could get lost forever. You should be thanking us instead of accusing us of theft,' my mother lied. We actually took the boat out of their boathouse after my mother broke the rusty lock with a brick. 'As for this cottage, have you spoken to the Millers lately?'

The man was obviously not used to dealing with someone like my mother. Few were. 'Well, no, but I do know he never rents this place out.'

'Well, do ya now?' My mother handed me the kittens and stood up to her five feet nine inches height, all long legs, curly amber hair and green piercing eyes, and walked towards the man and his whimpering wife. Inches away from the man's now level face, she said, 'I think you oughta talk to Mr. Miller before you come shooting your mouth off. People do change their minds.' Then she walked toward the cottage, shouting uncharacteristically mother-like, 'You kids better come on in now. The mosquitoes are biting.'

The next day the police car showed up. My mother talked to them for a bit in the driveway and then came back to the cottage and started packing things up. 'Go and call René. We're moving into town.'

René saw the police car and knew what was happening. When I found her, she was crying into Jimmy Reynolds' shoulder.

Our moving was okay by me because it was getting too cold in the damp cottage and school would be starting soon. The only sad part was leaving the cats. In the end, though, we kept one, all black with white paws, who we named Mr. Mittens. Mike hid him in his backpack, keeping him quiet by wrapping his mouth with cellotape. We had been living a week at the grey house in town before anyone even knew Mike had brought along Mr. Mittens.

I don't know how, but we managed to stay at the grey house for most of the rest of the year. This time, against my normal policy, I started to make a few friends at school. My best friend was a chubby girl called Veronicah. She lived in a big house near school and sometimes I'd go there and her mother would give us cookies and we'd play with Veronicah's doll house. But winter was coming and I could tell we were heading for trouble. My mother could be fun, a lot of fun, but when she started putting her Englebert Humperdink records on and sitting at the kitchen table smoking one cigarette after another, we all knew she was moving towards a black mood and we'd soon have to find my father to save us. I only hoped that she'd wait until Christmas because Veronicah and I had agreed to swap presents and I already knew what I would buy her. I'd seen it at the supermarket. A rhinestone tiara and little plastic shoes with rhinestone glued across the top. I knew she'd love them.

Thanksgiving weekend arrived and René bought a turkey. She woke up early and had the turkey in the oven before anyone else got up. At eleven o'clock, my mother still in bed, I heard a knock at the door. I was in the kitchen peeling potatoes as instructed by René. Mike, ever hopeful, shouted from elsewhere in the house, 'Daddy's here!' I left the potatoes to see who it was. At first I was confused. It was a crowd of people and at the front were Pastor Reynolds and Jimmy. People were holding boxes and grocery bags. They were smiling and I wasn't sure what they wanted. Then in the crowd I saw Veronicah and her cookie-giving mother and a man who I thought must be her father. Then René said, 'Well, Pastor Reynolds, isn't that so kind of you.' And she started taking the packages and I realised that they were full of food, tins of vegetables, bags of potatoes, another turkey. I watched as the boy who sat in front of me in class set down a huge tin of yams and then the janitor from school patted me and Mike on the head before setting down a box of old clothes.

And then Veronicah was there. I couldn't look at her. Her mother spoke and I heard nothing. I wanted to cry and scream and hide myself away forever. How could they do this to me? To us? How could René smile now that we were the 'poor people'? How could Veronicah want to be my friend anymore . . . why would she want some stupid plastic tiara and shoes from the 'poor girl'? Was that why her mother always gave me cookies?

They left just before my mother woke up. 'What the hell is this?' she asked René. She was pointing at all of the stuff piled up on the table.

'It's from the church, they wanted to help,' René said.

One by one my mother picked things from the boxes. I remember the first was a bottle of beet root salad, which she smashed against the white tiles across the kitchen. The purple-red juice splattered spectacularly. Tins hit furniture; bottles broke windows, potatoes rolled under the couch. 'Fuck your church!' she screamed, breathing hard and turning to René, and with one quick flick of the back of her hand René fell to the kitchen floor, her hand cut on a broken jar. My mother turned and disappeared into the icy Thanksgiving morning, no shoes, no coat, still in her nightgown.

I wrapped Rene's hand in a dish towel and called the phone number my father had given me when we left last time. He arrived in what seemed a very short time and we left the house without packing a thing.

The next time we saw my mother it was six or seven years after the do-gooders. She looked different, older and sadder. We never lived with her again.

I think about that day of the do-gooders sometimes. I wonder what happened to Rene's turkey that was in the oven and Mike wonders about Mr. Mittens. But René has never mentioned it again.

BAKING THE NATIONAL CAKE

Hilda Twongyeirwe

David sits staring at the report in front of him. Words wobble on the page. He pulls the next file closer and fingers the papers one by one. He twists his lips. His cheeks follow the twist of the lips. His face contorts. He has to be ready for the cabinet meeting at 11 AM. His accountability report is one of the two major items on the agenda. He feels that despite the input from the Permanent Secretary and the Chief Accountant, he still has not nailed down its details the way he should. Yet, because of the second major item - The Succession to Presidency Bill, he cannot concentrate to tie up the ends of the report. To nail it down to the appreciation of the President.

David taps his Parker pen on the page in front of him. He reads from one line to the next and back to the beginning. He looks at the papers and the words form a strange pattern against the white background. He wants to command his mind not to stray but he lacks the will to do so. The contentious issue of Succession to the Presidency Bill occupies the bigger part of his mind. As Minister for Presidency, he feels like an altar boy - watching the priest swig the wine while he waits to receive and wipe clean the empty Eucharist Chalice cup - tuck it away in the Holy Box. Do the priests ever care that the altar boy too might desire the taste of wine? That he might even be tempted to steal the wine in the absence of the priest? David had smelt and desired the taste of the Presidency too long. Now was the time. Ripe. To take his turn at it...

He places his hand on his left breast to wish away the sensations raving from within. The accountability report he is working on could cost the country billions of money if he does not handle it well. In fact, donors have already warned of an economic war if the government does not provide proper accountability. But who cares? For twenty-five years David has faithfully worked for the Republic of Kabira. For twenty-five years he has cared about nothing but the image of Kabira; first as Member of Parliament, then Minister of State for Ministry of Public Service, and now Minister for Presidency. But what do the President and his Vice-President do? Trot the globe, while he, David, does their work and also takes care of covering their tracks. They leave for two-day conferences and stay away for weeks. It is David that ensures that the accounts are balanced to include the nonofficial days. Do they think I am allergic to international travels?

Part of this current accountability report includes one of the VP's recent trips on 'Government Business.' The VP took his mistress on a shopping spree in London. When it was discovered that all her expenses were paid for by taxpayers' money, the VP asked David to quickly dispel the rumour by creating a ghost VIP from the Office of the President who supposedly traveled with the VP. David told him it was not easy, but the VP did not take him seriously. Now everything was back on his desk. More explanations were still being demanded by both the Auditor General and the donors. He remembers the time when The Daily Eye reported that the President's maternal aunt had used the Presidential jet to attend her daughter's wedding in France; it was David who accounted for that whole trip. 'They seem to think I am a magician,' David told his wife one evening as he cracked his head over a report.

'Maybe if you were President you too would need someone to cover up for you. Maybe that's the reason you are Minister for Presidency,' she challenged.

'This is a public office, not the President's personal office.'

'You seem to have no choice, so stop complaining.'

But David was tired of everything. And there were things he could not even share with his wife. Like when Mistress No. 5 threatened to kill the President and locked him up in her room for over an hour, it was David that he phoned to help sort it out.

'These women will kill you Sir,' David told him.

'It was a small issue.'

'I know Sir. But stop going to their homes.'

'And then?'

'And then what?'

'Exactly. And then what?'

'Sir, you can work it out differently.'

'Good. Then work it out and let me know. Treat the matter with utmost urgency.' David wanted to tell him that was not part of his job description, but he kept quiet. In a few days, a house was ready; PPMH - The President's Private Meditation House.

Sometimes David saw the hunger that lingered in these women's eyes. He knew most of them perhaps just wanted the President's money and status, not his sexual prowess. But because the President made all of them sign a secrecy oath, they were not supposed to 'see' any other man unless the President was dead. That was one of the clauses in the secrecy oath. David always wondered whether the President would do anything to them if they broke the oath. And some of them had his children. And did they all keep the oath any way? Like Mistress No1 - She was a head-turner. She was brainy too. Her Shipping Company was among the most successful in the country. In her mid fifties her springy walk still massaged the earth. Her husky voice sounded as if she spoke from a warm fluffy bed all the time. She was one woman that made David cross his legs to hide his raging hormones. Every time he chanced at her, he wished sex was like a handshake – grab a hand from anywhere without any restrictions. Or a cup of coffee which could be picked at ease from any restaurant or kitchen. He would then dash into her house as many times as he wished, sip her sweet scented coffee and leave in one fulfilled piece. But a handshake was a handshake. A cup of coffee was a cup of coffee. Sex was sex. No meeting point whatsoever.

David shoves the files aside. He pushes back his chair and stands up. He walks to the water dispenser to the left of his desk. He fills a paper cup with lukewarm water and downs it in one gulp. He does not like the taste.

He walks back towards his desk, crushes the disposable cup in his left hand, and smiles wryly at the crumpled paper. It is the VP in his hands. He throws him in the trashcan. His mind briefly turns to his administrative assistant. He has repeatedly told him to requisition another trashcan to place near the water cooler so that he can throw away the disposable cups right there. It bothers him to throw them in the trash basket near his desk. And he prefers the little brown trash basket for used cups in the VP's office. But his Administrative Assistant keeps forgetting. The man is very forgetful. He forgets most things, even those he is supposed to ensure that David must not forget. David makes a mental note in preparation for the next Staff Performance Review.

David stares at the Accountability Report again, but he does not sit down to continue with it. Instead, he opens the door and walks into the corridor towards the VP's office. 'Maybe he can advise on the London trip, he hisses as he heads to the office. He lingers in front of the door. He can hear muffled voices inside. David suspects that he might be on phone speaking to the President, back-biting other ministers, or soliciting support from colleagues, as he always did with David. He listens briefly but does not make out anything.

He feels like opening the door and stuffing the VP into one of the old closets, where he would be discovered a week or so later. A tingling sensation creeps inside his nose. His lips tighten over his teeth. As emotions begin to overtake him, he hears movement inside the room. The visitor or whoever it is, is getting up. David hurries off towards the end of the corridor, stretching his long arms and legs in an exaggerated manner. He then turns and heads back towards his office.

'That's some good exercise,' Badru, the Presidential Adviser on Press Matters says.

'Stretching my limbs a little,' David flashes him a smile.

'You wanted the VP?'

'No. Why?'

'I thought you stopped at his door.'

'Ah. Did I? No. As I said, I was just stretching my legs. Had not got up from my desk since I entered that office this morning.'

'I hear you have a cabinet meeting this morning?'

'Yes, we do. Why?'

I just asked because—'

'Ah. Okay. Yes.' David interrupts him and walks away back into his office. He knows Badru very well. He knows that he is not just asking but he does not pursue the thought. He does not want to. He is a green snake in green grass. But David likes him. At least he rustles in the grass and you notice his presence. Other snakes just spring before you notice them. Badru is not part of the cabinet but he knows more about what goes on in cabinet circles than the ministers themselves do. The fact that he does not have an official office does not stop him from being at the government hill almost every day. And it is rumored that he is the President's ear. But other people say that the President does not trust him entirely. David does not, either. He is dangerous but helpful at the same time. When David needs information, he just says one word and stories tumble out.

David reaches for the inner door that leads into his restroom. He does not have any urge to use restroom but he likes the idea of just being there for a little while.

In there, he is able to think uninterrupted, or not think at all. In there, he does not have to try to please anyone, not even the President. In there, he does not have to hide his true feelings towards the VP. He unzips his navy blue trousers. As a little urine trickles into the bowl, an image of the VP forms in his mind. The VP's face is the toilet bowl. As David shakes the last drops off his member, he wonders how the President came to consider Jacob for Vice-President. Jacob is an imbecile. Almost senile. Maybe that is the reason he was chosen. A right hand man that would offer no competition.

He hears a knock on the door and hurries out of the rest room.

'Come in.'

No one enters. Perhaps the knock was on another door along the corridor. He dismisses the thought as he turns to the Donors' Graft and Assessment Paper on the desk. As he turns the pages, he remembers the President's directive. 'Read the paper and analyse it, then prepare a defense report which will be discussed in cabinet before it is presented to the donor group. Do not give any information to the press,' the President had said. 'If they call, tell them you have not seen the donors' paper yet. You know them. They will call and press for information. That is certain. Do not tell them anything. We do not want information spreading without control.'

'Yes, Your Excellency.'

'Just tell them that you will hold a press

conference as soon as the report gets into your hands. OK?'

'Yes, Your Excellency.'

'The rest, you know what to do and what not to do.'

'I do, Your Excellency.'

'Perfect.'

David picks up his pen and starts to scan the paper. His lips twist as he underlines some statements.

He has keenly followed the speculation in the press and the rumors among cabinet ministers about the likely successor to the President. He taps his foot several times on the ground as he ponders the number of times the VP came out at the top of the list. Only once was David's name mentioned among the potential candidates. At that time he had not thought much about it. Shortly after that, there was a press survey in which he was voted the most honest cabinet minister of Kabira. Whereas many ministers were named in several scandals, David's name remained clean. He was happy with himself. He felt good that his fellow countrymen thought warmly about him. That's when the seed was planted. Now he does not just want to be the most honest Cabinet Minister - he wants to be the President. He has done a lot for the country already. Being President would be his just reward. After all, isn't it what we do today that determines what we become tomorrow?

David stretches his legs and shakes them. The Succession to Presidency Bill sits in his stomach like a hundred-ton stone. The bill is to determine many things: whether the President should name a successor, whether the electorate should vote for potential candidates, whether potential candidates can freely declare their interest, whether the country should remain a one-party state, and a lot more. But even without the succession bill, the rumbles of rumor and speculation are already shaking up things. It is not easy to predict a country that has had one president for 25 years – winning five elections.

What is clear to David, and the rest of the people of Kabira, is that the President will not run for election this time. He has said it himself several times. 'Now that I have built a peaceful state and successful economy, I would like to retire and give others the chance to prove themselves,' he says at almost every meeting and gathering.

David hopes that the President is aware of his potential. If he names me as his possible successor, all his supporters will rally behind me. But the imbecile VP has asked me for support. David remembers the day the VP called him to his office promising to discuss something very important for both of them. David's blood pressure had shot up that week, but he cancelled his appointment with the physician to be in the VP's office on time.

'What I need to discuss with you is something very important for both of us.' he told him.

'Very important.

'Yes. For both of us.'

When David entered the office, the VP secured the door behind him.

'You see, son, our President is retiring soon,' the VP said, rubbing his protruding stomach as if it had a burning sensation he was trying to soothe.

'Yes, His Excellency has said so. It is good that he is not running for office again in the next elections. That is very honourable of him. Kabira has kept its eggs in only one basket for too long. We need new leaders to come up. It is a good thing that the President will now retire. And his age – 85 years is no mean achievement.'

'That's the point my son. So what do you think?'

'I think we need new blood. Young blood—'

'Yes and no.'

'Aah. What were you thinking?'

'You see, the President is Muslim.'

'Yes, Sir.'

'You and I are Christians.'

'Hmm. Hmm. Yes Sir. Yes sir.'

'We have had twenty-five years of Islamic rule!'

'That is true Sir. That is true. So what were you thinking Sir?'

'Exactly. That is why I called you here.'

'I am listening, Sir.'

'Like I said, you and I are Christians. We have to

do something. We have to strategise on how to represent our lot effectively. We are their eyes and ears. Where they are not, we are.'

'Hmm . . . hmm . . . hmm. Yes Sir. I agree with you.'

'I am happy you do. And so, who do you think is the best candidate to replace His Excellency other than the man who has deputised him for over ten years? We have to share the National Cake too.'

The VP's use of the word 'we,' as if they were husband and wife, irritated David. He wanted to tell the VP to be equally as enthusiastic about baking the National Cake as he was about sharing it, but he joined the VP in loud laughter, the kind shared by people who are not sure of how to laugh together.

'But you see, Sir, it might not be as easy as you think. There might be many people interested in this cake, as you call it,' David responded in between spasms of forced laughter. After a brief silence, he leaned forward and said, 'It might not be about religion, region, or even age.' The word 'age' came out of his pursed lips with precision. To end the conversation, he added, 'Sir, I have always supported you, not just because we share a religion but because I believe in your abilities.'

'Will you support me in this?'

'If you ask me to.'

The VP's assumptions made David sick to the ends of his toes and the tips of his hair.

Another time, when they were in a meeting to form a committee to coordinate the Kabira Rapid Response Initiative (KRRI), David was riding waves of uncertainty, waiting for someone to nominate him then he received a note from the VP. David smiled as he opened the note. He was grateful to the VP for thinking about him at least this once. His smile stretched his lips and his hairline and it shone into his eyes. He felt like a child whose selfish big brother had finally acknowledged and rewarded. He lowered his eyes and read the note. After reading, he took a deep breath and emptied his face of all expression before he looked up at the VP. The note was brief and to the point. 'David, please nominate me. I would like to serve on this committee. Thank you.' David had never felt his arm so heavy and his tongue so thick as he nominated Jacob. As soon as he volunteered the name, he closed his eyes in a quick prayer. God, let no one second this nomination. The imbecile is like a bottomless pit. Wanting more and more and more. Put a stop to this dear Lord. Amen. Not only was the VP seconded, he became Chairperson of the committee as well. At the end of the meeting, the VP walked over to David and said, 'Son, I saw you praying for me after you nominated me. Thank you very much. I am so proud of you.'

'Thank you Sir,' David answered, his lips twisted in a wry smile.

They shook hands.

Imbecile.

David looks at his BlackBerry. The time icon flashes. An hour and a half have shot past since he got into office. He has done nothing substantial. He pulls the Accountability Report closer and remembers the words of Dr. Joseph Murphy, in his Power of the Subconscious Mind: People have the power to change their thought patterns. He takes a deep breath and invites his mind to refocus. He wonders how much money his wife spent on each acclaimed self help and inspirational books. They never seemed to work for him. 'The meeting is crucial. I must refocus!' he says as he shakes his fist in frustration.

At eleven o'clock, David sits in the committee room ready for his presentation. His immaculate white shirt and blue bow tie belie his anxiety. In the committee room, the President and a few members of the Cabinet are already seated.

Today the whole cabinet is here. David notices that when they talk, their words do not come from their depths. They come from their lips, marred with anxiety. The Donors' Graft and Assessment Paper and the Succession Bill are what sit deeper.

David watches the President as he stands up to address the House. As usual, he starts with comments on the growing economy and how important it is for leaders to work together and to support one another in order for the nation to progress. David listens as the President talks about the unstable global political and economic climate and adds that Kabira needs leaders who will guide the nation through this instability.

'For that matter, I have made several consultations with very reliable political analysts both within and outside Kabira and they have all advised that at the moment it is unwise to table the Succession to the Presidency Bill. It is better that the situation stabilises first, before we subject the Developing Nation of Kabira to any big changes.'

David watches members of the house nod their heads in slow motion. He is not sure whether on their part; it is in agreement, disapproval or in confusion.

'Our plate is already full.' The President clears his throat and continues, 'It is therefore important that I let you know that today we shall not discuss the Succession to Presidency Bill. Again, I have consulted and we have agreed that when the time comes, whoever among you wants to run for office, you will battle it out with your opponents. It is only your works that will make you President of this great nation.' David feels an urge to ask the President when the time will come, but he does not. Certain statements are safer left unspoken.

'In addition, I would like you to know that people of Kabira have asked me to run for president for another term to allow this government to consolidate the economy and stabilise the nation more, but of course, I have not said yes yet. They have promised to give me votes as usual. Their reasoning is that they do not want to see all that we have worked hard for go down the drain under irresponsible leadership. No. The issue is, I am not sure I want to retain presidency for the next five years. I feel tired and I feel I have already done my share in building the nation. But we shall see when the time comes. Of course I will put the Nation's needs before my personal needs. As you are all aware, I get my energy from you, from the people of Kabira. If they say so, who am I to say; no, I won't lead you?' Again, as I said, I have not said yes yet.

David places his right hand on the files in front of him while his left hand plays with his parker pen again. He looks around but the faces in the room show no emotion. Even the VP's face is blank, save for the little beads of sweat claiming his forehead and his nose despite the cool morning. David wants to say to the President that running for elections again did not quite guarantee him a win. I might surprise him for example. But no. I have watched the pattern. For twenty five years. Consolidating. Consolidation. Consolidation. consolidation. Consolidation.

David's eyes shift from the VP and float through to the blue sky outside the window on his left. A flock of white birds forms a string and is moving in one direction across the horizon. The egrets flip their wings in unison and glide through the air with ease. He wonders how the lead bird got to the front and whether the birds following are aware of where the lead bird is taking them. Suddenly the birds change direction. The bird at the tail of the string takes lead. The rest follow, flip flapping their wings. Flip flapping. A few birds linger behind above trees and shrubs before swinging back into the curve. Others simply stay outside the curve but they do not go away. They are part of the flock. Somehow.

'For now, we shall look at the Donors' Graft and Assessment Paper and see what Hon. David Okello has for us. Hon. Okello, you have the floor.' David is still looking through the window at the white birds.

'Mr Okello, the floor is yours,' the President repeats.

When David turns, he wants to scream at the president… Imbecile! Instead, he smiles.

'Thank you, Mr. President,' he says, stepping forward to the podium.

SHORTCUT

Sylvia Schlettwein

'Are you sure this is a shortcut? Why is the GPS not showing a track?'

'It's not on the GPS, but it's a shortcut. Edgar told me about it. They drove here when they went on their last trip with Stefan and them.'

'Oh really. And they would know, your expat friends. They always come and ask us for advice and now you tell me they're the experts on shortcuts in the Namibian bush. Don't make me laugh.'

'Would you like to direct us?'

'No, I trust you. This just doesn't look like a shortcut to me. More like a longcut.'

#

I look at how the arrow representing our car moves across the otherwise grey GPS screen. I hate it when Thomas does this. I know my sense of direction is bad. I have to phone my friends to get directions every time I visit them, every vacation at the sea I still lose my way in Swakopmund, I aimlessly drive in circles before I find my sister's home that I have looked for and found many times before, I study the roadmap for hours before driving to visit my aunt and uncle on the farm and when I'm on the way I have to pull up to the picnic spots next to the road to check on the map whether I haven't missed a turnoff. I know Thomas's sense of direction is excellent and he knows how to read a map, on paper or GPS. I leave the route planning and navigation entirely up to him when we go on our off-road safari trips. When I'm on holiday, I don't want to stress with something I'm hopeless at. I know that I am in no position to judge, but I hate it when he takes so-called shortcuts that make that GPS arrow crawl into grey nowhere.

'Daddy, are we lost?' Mara enquires from the back.

'What? Are we lost?' Lia asks from the middle backseat.

'No, we're just taking a shortcut,' Thomas reassures our two eldest daughters.

'What's a shortcut?' Anne, the youngest, wants to know.

'You took the shortcut, Thomas. You explain it.' I look out the side window to demonstrate that I have left the conversation.

'I'm driving and you're better at explai . . . Shit!'

Massive horns, brown with white speckles, big

moist brown eyes, dung ball in mid air between lifted tail and hard ground. Too late. Bang. The picture of the cow disappears as the windscreen morphs into a splintery mosaic. Standstill. Silence. Three distinctive cries from the back. I turn around. Three little girls in tears. No blood. Relief.

'We've hit a cow.' Thomas can talk. Relief.

Before I can say anything, reach out my hands to touch everybody, feel that everybody is alive, the car is full of strange faces and babbling voices. Otjiherero, I recognise the familiar language that I can't speak. You've wanted to learn Otjiherero or Ovambo for a long time. Why don't you? The thought flashes through my dazed brain. I don't know how, but in what seems a few seconds we are outside our four-by-four. Massive horns, brown with white speckles, big white eyeballs, pieces of flesh and hide on our bulbar and smashed bonnet. Too late. Cooler water, oil and cow's blood flow together, form a puddle that stands unabsorbed on the dry, dirty-white soil.

'Do we have cell phone reception?' Thomas's voice sounds as though it has worked its way through thick clouds of dust. I feel for my cell phone in my pocket. It's still there, I flip it open—no connection.

'No, we don't. Surprise!'

'Telephone?' I ask into the semi-circle of men around us.

One of them nods and points into the landscape.

'Far?' Thomas asks.

The men weigh their heads from left to right, shrug their shoulders, then decide to nod and say: 'Ja, far. Farm.'

'Car? Who can take me?'

'No car.' A lean young man with dancing eyes, so dark they don't seem to have pupils, points at a rusty Suzuki cadaver in front of one of the metal shacks. 'I take you. I'm Kaushimo. You pay me?' Kaushimo extends his milk chocolate hand towards Thomas who takes it and nods.

'We have no choice.' Thomas rubs his shaved head. 'You stay here with the kids. I go to the farmhouse with this guy. I'll phone your parents to pick us up and tow the car to Windhoek.'

'How will they know where to find us?'

'I'll tell your father how we drove. I still remember. And the farmer will be able to direct us. I hope he's prepared to drive me back here. I'll pitch the tent with you before I leave. Please pack a water bottle and something to eat for me. I'll take my small rucksack. There's more than enough food and water in the car for you.'

'I know that. I packed it myself.' I don't want to pick a fight with Thomas in this situation, but I have a feeling that he's enjoying this: Man goes out on treacherous hike to get wife and kids out of desperate situation. Man ensures wife and kids have shelter before man sets out on treacherous hike. Wife lovingly prepares provisions for brave man. Wife and kids bid husband and father farewell with tears in their eyes and hope in their hearts. Nobody mentions that man got wife and kids into desperate situation, or so wife feels.

We pitch the tent next to an acacia that has not made it to the size of a tree you can pitch your tent under. It takes us less than ten minutes; we have our wordless routine despite the shock and the anger lodged in my throat. As we hook the tent body onto the tent poles, I see droplets of sweat pushing out on Thomas's naked scalp on which light brown patches and off-white skin arrange themselves in map-like patterns. I remind him to put on a cap and apply sunscreen before he leaves.

'Thank you for reminding me.' Thomas smiles at me and runs his index finger over my left cheek. 'Sometimes I do get the impression that you care for me,' he mocks and adds: 'If I'm not back by tomorrow evening, you'll have to send somebody to look for me.' The anger glides down my throat, my stomach will take care of it. I smile at Thomas. The girls and I kiss Thomas goodbye. We look on till Thomas and Kaushimo merge into the landscape.

I'm not happy about the colourful dot that loosens itself from the landscape, becomes bigger and bigger and morphs into an old woman in full Herero garb next to us where we sit in front of our tent. She has chosen a pink and green flowery material for her headscarf and the ample long sleeved, floor length dress. I don't want to talk to strangers right now. Was it her cow that we hit? Wife has to negotiate price for dead cow in absence of brave man in search of telephone.

'Good afternoon,' she greets. 'How are you? Welcome.'

'Thank you. I'm sorry about the cow. We will pay you for it.'

She shrugs. 'Not my cow. Your man can make an offer to the chief when he comes back. I'm Gustafine,' she says and settles herself on the ground next to us.

'I'm Sofia. And these are Mara, Lia and Anne.'

'Omakaia?' I ask when she pulls out a pipe from the depth of her skirt folds. I offer her a cigarette.

'No, I have my own tobacco. All yours?' She points at the girls.

'Yes, all mine.' I detect mother's pride in my voice and feel a smile spreading over my face. She slowly nods her head three times before the dark brown eye beads hidden in the wrinkles of her eyelids find my eyes.

'All one man?'

'Yes, all one man. And you? Do you have children, grandchildren?'

'Yes, many. Five sons, four daughters, many grandchildren.'

'That's a lot!' Mara's eyes widen as she looks up

to Gustafine. 'And why do you speak German?' It's only now that I realise Gustafine has been talking in German and that I have responded automatically. Before I can repeat Mara's question, Gustafine asks:

'Do you know old Mister Krug?'

'I've heard the name, I think. Old German family in Namibia, isn't it?'

'Yes. Old German family. Only German with a farm in the area. I used to work there. Those were good times. I was young, beautiful, healthy. We got milk and meat, sugar and tobacco.' On this cue she pulls from the folds of her dress a pouch with Dingler's Black and White Tobacco and pours some tobacco into the pipe. I light a cigarette and offer her a light, then watch her nostrils flare and her cheeks go hollow and plump and hollow and plump as she draws on the pipe to get the tobacco burning. 'Aaaah,' she sighs at last, and lets the smoke billow from her nostrils and mouth. I expect it to come out of her ears as well, but it doesn't. I draw on my cigarette and manage to blow some smoke rings. Anne giggles and tries to push her arms through them. Mara shakes her sensible blonde head and says:

'You know smoking is bad for you. Daddy has told you many times.' She turns to Gustafine. 'My daddy has stopped smoking, you know.'

Gustafine cackles and cocks her head, then rubs her neck, which reminds me of a turtle's, thin and wrinkly.

'Krug was like that. First he gave me tobacco and smoked it with me, then he stopped. But he knew I would come to ask for tobacco. I liked the taste too much. And he liked the taste of my mouth after tobacco.'

Lia looks up from the drawing she has scratched into the sand with a dry stick. 'What do you mean he liked the taste of your mouth after tobacco?' she asks. 'Did he eat you?'

I blush and try to avoid Gustafine's eyes. She gives another smoky laugh, sucks on her pipe, and strokes Lia's head. 'Yes, he ate me,' she said. 'Like you eat meat from a bone. And he licked me. Like you lick the bone that has given you such good meat. This bone gave him five children, two daughters and three sons. They've all left, too boring here. Except Kaushimo, my youngest child from Krug. I don't have to share the tobacco and sugar he sends with the other of Krug's kids anymore. I only share with Kaushimo and my Herero kids, two daughters, two sons, but I don't give the daughters tobacco. It's not good if a woman smokes.'

I choke on my smoke and cough.

'See. It's not good if a woman smokes.' Her flowery headscarf horns shudder in my direction as she nods to her words.

'My husband doesn't mind,' I lie.

'You'll see. He'll chase you away and get another woman. A black one. Men like swopping colours. Krug sent me away when a white woman found him. One who didn't smoke. He didn't even want his children anymore. Although they were so beautiful. Like coffee with milk and sugar, he used to say.'

'You can't see sugar in coffee!' Anna waves a little index finger.

'Oh yes, you can.' Gustafine lifts her wiry eyebrows. 'Especially if it's brown sugar, my girl. My pipe is finished. I shall go now. Don't worry, you'll be safe here, even at night. I'll send one of my sons to watch.' She takes my hands into hers and says: 'Go well.' I squeeze her hands. 'Thank you. Go well, Gustafine.' I help her up and we watch the dust spiral around the hem of her dress as she wanders off to the shacks.

'She was funny.' Mara says.

'I liked her.' Lia says.

'She's a grandma.' Anne says.

The next morning we awake at the hum of a car engine and the clunk of tyres meeting stones. I get out of the tent and see a blue bakkie approaching. Shoulder portrait of Thomas and a grey-haired, bearded man behind the windscreen. Kaushimo like a statue on the back of the bakkie. They stop next to our tent. Thomas and the driver get out of the car, Kaushimo jumps from the back, lands on his feet in a cat-like motion. Thomas and I hug each other.

'I'm so glad you're back safe.'

'Me too. Everything is fine. Your father is on his way. We'll leave the car here. Insurance will arrange for towage. The car's a write-off, I guess.'

'Yes, but the main thing is that you're all unharmed,' the greybeard says.

'Definitely. Sofia, this is Alfred Krug.'

We shake hands. Farmer's vice-like handshake that paralyses the hand such that you cannot reciprocate. 'Angenehm. Pleased to meet you. Thank you for helping us,' I say.

'No problem. You're lucky you came across Kaushimo. He knows his way around here and he's a good man. Sometimes you don't know with these people.'

'Oh, really. You know him well then?'

'Yes, he sometimes comes to work on my farm. Fences and stuff. He's almost like family.' Krug turns to Kaushimo, says something in Otjiherero. Kaushimo nods like an automaton and says, 'I go now. Go well.'

'Go well and thank you.' Thomas lifts a greeting hand. Kaushimo does the same and saunters off.

'I also have to be off. My wife and son are waiting for me back at the farm. Take care.' Another tight-gripping handshake and Krug is behind the steering wheel. He starts the engine. We can still hear the roar of the bakkie long after it is no longer visible between the grey hills. Thomas puts his arm around my shoulders and says, 'Let's have breakfast and pack up the tent. Your father should be here in three hours or so.'

The girls hang onto Thomas's arms, pull at his

shirt and shorts. 'It was a long wait, Daddy, but it wasn't so bad. An old woman came and smoked with Mommy and told us strange stories,' Lia informs him. I wait for Thomas to make a remark about the smoking, but he doesn't.

In the safety of my father's 'truck,' as he refers to it, the girls fall asleep to engine's hum and the diesel fumes. 'Where did you actually call from?' my father asks Thomas.

'From a farm, I don't remember the name. The farmer's name is Alfred Krug. We had to walk for about six hours from where you picked us up.'

'That farmer seems to be well known in the area,' I add. 'Gustafine, the old woman the kids talked about, told us of a man called Krug. She used to work on his farm.'

'Oh, really? What a coincidence. Where was she when we had the accident? I'm sure she would have known the shortest way on foot back to the farm. I had a feeling that Kaushimo guy I went with didn't take the shortest path.'

'Yes, pity you missed her. But Kaushimo is her son, he'd know the way.' I look at our children, Mara, Lia and Anne, peacefully asleep in their seats. I squeeze Thomas's shoulders from behind and say, 'Still, if Gustafine would have taken you, I'm sure she would have known about a shortcut.'

Notes on Authors

Anyango Doreen is a Ugandan biotechnologist and lover of books. She has always sought to escape the drudgery of everyday life through the written word-devouring other people's brilliant tales long before she had the courage to come up with some of her own. Her work of fiction has appeared in several online publications. She lives in Kampala, Uganda.

Bolaji Odofin is a Nigerian writer and journalist.

Cheru-Mpambawashe Monica trained as a secondary school teacher and majored in English and Portuguese. She introduced college creative writers' magazine Panorama. She also worked in the media as a columnist, senior reporter and planning and lifestyle editor. She is a published writer of several short stories. Her short story collection, Chivi Sunsets, was published in 2011. She is a member of Zimbabwe Writers Association and is currently working on two novels.

Dhliwayo Mercy was born in November 1983. She is a Zimbabwean poet and emerging fiction writer. In 2011, her short story, Ango Leonard's Game, was amongst the 14 stories shortlisted for the Yvonne Vera Award (Zimbabwe). Her works of poetry have featured in various musical compilations. She is published online and in print.

Gardner Grace Neliya was born in the Katete district of Zambia. At school she particularly enjoyed English and Geography; subjects she has made full use of in her writing and working with children, teaching wildlife and conservation. She has strong feelings about the importance of humans living in balance with the rest of nature. Neliya is close to her family; amai (mother) of eight and ambuye (grandmother) of many. She lives in a suburb of Lusaka. Neliya is an active psycho-social counsellor and also works with church groups, particularly those who help the poor.

Karen Jennings is the author of Finding Soutbek and the short story collection Away from the Dead. She also edited the anthology of short stories entitled Feast, Famine and Potluck for Short Story Day Africa in 2013. Karen currently lives in Cape Town.

Kawuma Davina is a published writer of short stories. She lives and works in Kampala, Uganda. Davina is a member of FEMRITE.

Kiguwa Melissa is the author of Reveries of Longing. She is a blue writer, performer, a social critic, television and radio personality. Raised by a Haitian father and a Ugandan mother, Melissa considers herself an Afro-diasporic nomad. Much of her work is influenced by Migration, imperialism, gender, spirituality, sexuality and capitalism.

Kubuitsile Lauri is a full-time writer living in Botswana. She has published two detective novellas three children's books, three collections of short stories for children co-written with two other Batswana writers. She has published three romance novels with Sapphire Press; Kwaito Love, Can He Be The One?, and Mr Not Quite Good Enough. Kubuitsile was the 2007 winner of the BTA/ Anglo Platinum Short Story Contest and the recipient of the Botswana Ministry of Youth and Culture's Orange Botswerere Award for Creative Writing in the same year. In 2009 she won the Baobab Literary Prize (USA) in the junior category and in 2010 in the senior category. She was on the shortlist for the 2011 Caine Prize. Kubuitsile is married and have two teenage children

Lisa-Anne Julien was born and grew up in Trinidad and Tobago. In 1992 she moved to New York to study dance at the Alvin Ailey American Dance Centre and the Martha Graham School for Contemporary Dance. After 3 years in New York, Lisa left for London to complete degrees in development studies and social policy. To pay her tuition, she worked as a nursing assistant in a psychiatric hospital for 4 years. In 2002, Lisa moved to South Africa and has since worked as a researcher, writer and consultant in the field of gender and women's rights and HIV/ AIDS. She has written for a number of magazines as well as peer-reviewed journals. Lisa was one of ten finalists for the 2008 Women & Home Magazine South Africa short story competition and in November 2008 she was selected as a winner in the "Highly Commended" category of the Commonwealth Short Story competition of that year. Her novel, "More than Friends" was published by Nollybooks in 2010. She currently lives in Johannesburg.

Makhosazana Xaba is a writing fellow at the Wits School of Public Health, co-writing a book on nursing history in South Africa. She was a writing fellow at the Wits Institute for Social and Economic Research (WiSER) from May 2006 to April 2007 writing a biography of Helen Nontando Jabavu. She is the author of two poetry collections: these hands (Timbila, 2005) and Tongues of their Mothers (UKZN Press, 2008). She is a co-editor, with Karen Martin, of Queer Africa: New and Collected Fiction (MaThoko Books, 2013) and a collection of short stories, Running and other stories, wwas published in 2013 by Modjaji Books. She holds a Diploma in Journalism (with distinction) from Warner Lambertz School of Journalism, Berlin and an MA in Creative Writing (with distinction)

from Wits University. She is the winner of the 2005 Deon Hofmeyr Award for Creative Writing.

Nkansa Famia is an Ewe fiction writer, playwright, poet, blogger and social commentator who is constantly trying to parse the sites of contradiction in human identities. She is Ghanaian and works as a communications consultant. She believes that her writing was invaluably enriched by her time at the 4th FEMRITE residency and yearns to once again find mentorship, participate in a community of women writers and thrive in a safe space where she can develop her craft and hone her passion for writing the stories she would like to see about the people, places and experiences that she feels have been for too long invisible.

Nkwoma Masi Linda is from Rivers State, Nigeria. She has a certificate in Creative Writing and an Executive Masters Certificate in Project Management. Some of her works have appeared in the Sunday Tide and in an anthology of short stories. She is a member of the Association of Nigerian Authors (ANA)-Port Harcourt. She splits her time writing freelance, singing, running Sparrow Writers Club, and managing a printing business in Port Harcourt.

Olufunke Ogundimu was born on November 7, 1980. She lives in Lagos, Nigeria. She is a graduate of the University of Lagos. She is a public servant. She was a participant at the 2011 Farafina Trust Creative Writers' Workshop, Lagos. Her short story is forthcoming in an anthology by Nelson (Evans). She collects recipes and postage stamps. She is currently working on a collection of short stories.

Sylvia Schlettwein was born on 16 November 1975 in Omaruru, Namibia. She grew up in Stellenbosch, South Africa, Katima Mulilo, Namibia and Windhoek, Namibia. She holds a BA-Degree in German and French of the University of Cape Town. In 2000 she joined her future husband Jürgen Haag in Stuttgart, Germany where she continued to study German and French Language and Literature at the University of Stuttgart and the Ecole Normale Supérieure de Lettres et Sciences Humaines in Lyon, France. In 2002, she lived in Underberg, South Africa before she returned to Windhoek in 2003 where she worked as a travel agent for two years. From 2004 – 2006 she taught French and German at the Deutsche Höhere Privatschule in Windhoek. In February 2008 she opened her own language centre in Windhoek where she teaches German, English, Afrikaans and French to adults and children. Sylvia writes short fiction in English and German and poetry in German and Afrikaans. She received a Highly Commended award for her short story Framing the Nation in the 2010 Commonwealth Short Story Competition and her story To own a bed was published in The Bed Book of Short Stories (Modjaji 2010). Her German short stories and poems have been published and awarded in both Namibia and Germany. Sylvia lives in Windhoek with her husband and their three daughters Miriam, Lisa and Amelie.

Twongyeirwe Hilda is a founding member of FEMRITE. She has published children and adult fiction. Her short stories and poems appear in different anthologies and collections. She has authored and co-edited works which raise critical issues on gender-based and sexual violence, women and armed conflict, and female genital mutilation. Hilda serves on The African Asian Writers Union and the National Book Trust of Uganda Boards of Directors. She holds an MA in Public Administration and Management and B.A in Social Sciences from Makerere University. Currently she is the Executive Director of FEMRITE-Uganda Women Writers Association.

Printed in the United States
By Bookmasters